HOW TO
DESIGN & REMODEL
BATHROOMS

Created and designed
by the editorial staff
of ORTHO Books

Project Editor Anne Coolman
Writer William A. Henkin
Designer Christine Butterfield
Illustrator Rik Olson
Photographer Stephen Marley
Photographic Stylist Sara Slavin
Plan Drawings Diane Snow Crocker

Ortho Books

Publisher
Robert L. Iacopi

Editorial Director
Min S. Yee

Managing Editors
Anne Coolman
Michael D. Smith
Sally W. Smith

Production Manager
Ernie S. Tasaki

Editors
Jim Beley
Susan Lammers
Deni Stein

Design Coordinator
Darcie S. Furlan

System Managers
Christopher Banks
Mark Zielinski

Photographic Director
Alan Copeland

Photographers
Laurie A. Black
Richard A. Christman

Production Editors
Linda Bouchard
Alice Mace
Kate O'Keeffe

Asst. System Manager
William F. Yusavage

Chief Copy Editor
Rebecca Pepper

Photo Editors
Anne Dickson-Pederson
Pam Peirce

National Sales Manager
Garry P. Wellman

Sales Associate
Susan B. Boyle

Operations Director
William T. Pletcher

Operations Assistant
Gail L. Davis

Administrative Assistant
Georgiann Wright

Address all inquiries to
Ortho Books
Chevron Chemical Company
Consumer Products Division
575 Market Street
San Francisco, CA 94105

Chevron Chemical Company
575 Market Street, San Francisco, CA 94105

Front Cover

Like many of the newer bathrooms, this one is designed to give a sense of openness, light, and space. Nothing is hidden away. The custom shower needs no doors or curtain, the sliding glass doors open the room out, and the skylight opens the room up. A full-wall mirror expands the visual space of the bathroom even further. Because the outside patio is fully enclosed, the user can enjoy the indoor-outdoor feeling without losing a sense of privacy. In such an open room, details take on added significance. Here, handpainted ceramic basins and distinctive brass fittings for both washbasins and shower catch the eye. In addition, color—towels, flowers, and other accessories—can alter the look and feel of the room; it can be dressed up or down according to taste and mood.

Page 1

Utter simplicity is the key to this bathroom. Standard fixtures are featured as design elements, rather than being downplayed. Even the p-trap and shutoff valves add to the design with their stark symmetry. Wrap-around white tiles cover the floor, walls, *and* ceiling. Narrow aluminum blinds continue both the scale of the small tiles and the color of the fittings. And when you slide the mirror back to expose recessed shelves, you discover that the design extends to include intriguing art objects along with the basic necessities. The mirror, which stretches from wall to wall when closed, and the glass shower partition both extend the apparent space of this very small bathroom. Because the bathroom is totally white, introducing any color would create a dominant focal point, which might detract from the overall design. See page 24 for a look at the shower area.

Back Cover

Classic lines and custom details combine to give this odd-shaped room a soft, comfortable feeling. The two main functional areas are clearly defined by dividing them with a half-wall and by using different wood surfaces. The upper molding in the bath area contains the high-ceilinged space, and the unusually large single-pane window not only provides an unobstructed view of the hills but is scaled to the height of the walls. Subtly patterned beige paper softens the walls, and the window and tub surround trim repeat the lighter wood color of the floor. The net effect is a cozy, quiet bathing niche in what could have been a vague, awkward space. Washbasins and counter top take on a touch of elegance with the use of synthetic marble and detailed brass fittings. To see other details of this bathroom, turn to page 19.

Acknowledgments

See page 96.

HOW TO
DESIGN & REMODEL
BATHROOMS

GETTING STARTED

Take a closer look at
the bathroom you already have.
Use the Bathroom Survey to help you assess
your needs and establish your priorities.
Then draw up your Existing Plan as
a foundation for creating the
bathroom you really want.

Why are you holding this book in your hands? Presumably, you are thinking of remodeling your bathroom, and you want some ideas, assistance, and guidance. If so, you've come to the right place.

Most people who remodel their bathrooms do so for one of four reasons: They want more space; they want to modernize the look, feel, or function of the room; they start to make a single change, such as replacing a broken toilet, and then decide to make a more substantial alteration; or they have just grown tired of the way their bathroom looks and want a change for the sake of change itself. Whatever your reason may be for thinking about remodeling your bathroom, there is some specific information you ought to have in order to translate your ideas into reality in the best possible way. How to get and use that information is what this book is about.

The book is not intended to tell you everything there is to know about bathroom design and remodeling or tell you how to accomplish every possible task you might want to undertake. For example, if you need to dig into your walls and floors for deep-seated plumbing or electrical jobs, such as diverting your pipes, wires, and vents, you will find the substantive answer to your questions in Ortho's books, *Basic Plumbing Techniques* and *Basic Wiring Techniques*. This book, however, will help you decide whether those jobs are necessary.

Remodeling an ordinary bathroom can be a simple matter of changing the surface materials. The only structural alteration in this previously unremarkable room of standard dimensions was the installation of a shower stall, using glass walls to avoid a claustrophobic effect. The bathroom's elegance is achieved with new wall and floor treatments combining synthetic marble with soft peach wallpaper, wall-to-wall carpeting, and trim louvered shutters — a totally new look at a modest cost.

Remodeling your bathroom is actually a straightforward series of steps:

1. Assess your present bathroom. While you're gathering new ideas, take a closer look at the bathroom you already have. The Bathroom Survey and the Existing Plan on pages 8 and 10 in this chapter will help you develop a composite of information about your bathroom that will simplify all the stages of your remodeling project.

2. Define your style. Chapter Two outlines the general process of designing a bathroom and includes photographic displays of well-designed bathrooms in a wide variety of styles. Knowing the general direction you want your design style to take will help you make material selections and other design decisions.

3. Draw up a plan. Chapter Three shows you how to draw up a specific bathroom plan of your own. An example of ten different floor plans for one sample bathroom shows you how to look at your space in new ways. Illustrations of scale, line, and color help you tie your design together. Charts categorize the vast array of products and materials on today's market, speeding the process of choosing new bathroom elements. And detailed guidelines help you organize the phases of your project, list the materials you'll need, estimate your costs and time, and outline the work you want to subcontract.

4. Take out the old. Chapter Four provides specific instructions for removing the fixtures, fittings, surface coverings, and cabinetry in your present bathroom.

5. Install the new. Chapter Five provides step-by-step instructions and illustrations for installing all your new bathroom elements.

If you're eager to get going, you may be tempted to turn directly to Chapter Four and start ripping out your old fixtures. Don't. One man took out his washbasin and then waited three months for a replacement. Good planning will save you time, money, and disappointment; and planning is what these first three chapters are all about.

PROJECT OVERVIEW

At the beginning of any major project, it helps to have an overview of some of the issues you'll be dealing with. In this case, major issues include budget, schedules, plumbing, wiring, and what "doing it yourself" actually means. You'll find a discussion of these issues on these two pages.

Budget

The amount of money you spend remodeling your bathroom depends on what you want and how much you want it. An enameled steel or molded fiberglass bathtub costs between $100 and $500. On the other hand tubs made of marble and onyx with gold-covered fittings can cost more than $5000. If you select inexpensive materials and do virtually all the work yourself, you can completely remodel a standard bathroom for well under $1000. But you can just as easily spend $10,000 or more for the same job if you buy costly materials and hire a lot of professional assistance. Before you begin, you should have some idea of what you're willing to spend. Then to arrive at a ballpark figure of what your remodeling will actually cost, you have to determine what changes you want to make. When you've come up with some alternative plans, you can hire a general contractor to make an estimate or you can make your own (see page 48). The results may send you back to the drawing board, but it is only by moving back and forth between plans and estimates that you will be able to set a budget and stay within its limits.

Schedules

The amount of time a job will take depends on the complexity of the job and the skill of the person doing it. You can remove and replace a toilet in an hour if you know what you're doing and have already received your replacement fixture. On the other hand there is no limit to the amount of time you can spend shopping or correcting your mistakes if you are unprepared. Completely remodeling a standard bathroom will take at least a couple of weeks, and can easily take several months if you're doing your own work at night and on weekends. To develop a reliable remodeling schedule, you must take into consideration your planning and shopping time as well as delivery times for special-order fixtures. As with costs, you will be unable to work up any sort of realistic schedule until you know what you want to accomplish. Both schedules and costs are discussed in more detail on pages 48 and 52.

Doing It Yourself

Doing your own bathroom remodeling can mean making all the design decisions, working out the plans, and managing the overall project without ever laying hammer to nail or picking up a single wrench. Or it can mean relying on outside design assistance while pulling out the old fixtures with your own two hands and installing every new item from the smallest piece of tile to the largest bathtub. And, of course, it can mean any sort of role in between. You are the one who defines what "doing it yourself" means. The most important part is knowing what your skills are and when you need help.

Building Permits

Whether or not you'll need a building permit depends on your local codes. The determining factor may be the total cost of the project, the extent of the work you do, or both. In many areas you can make up to $750 worth of changes in your house without obtaining a permit—as long as you don't substantially alter your plumbing, heating, or wiring systems. You can find out what the criteria are in your community by calling your Building Inspection office. They will also tell you whether or not you need prior approval by another agency. For example, in some communities bathroom remodeling projects require approval by the sanitation department. If you need a permit, you'll want to know what plans you'll need to supply, how many and in what form, and if and when inspections will be required. Generally, the department is checking to ensure that you are meeting code requirements such as proper clearances around fixtures. Despite the potential for a lot of extra running around, the Building Inspection office can be a good source of information. When you actually get into the work and find that you need help with a particular aspect of your project, you may find that you'll welcome their assistance.

Plumbing and Wiring Changes

In any bathroom remodeling project, there is always the potential for extensive and costly plumbing and wiring changes. On the other hand you may not realize how extensively you can alter both the size and look of your bathroom by tapping into existing lines or even by leaving your fixtures exactly where they are right now. Further, the cost of plumbing changes may be determined more by access to the lines than by the change itself. No one change—even a plumbing or wiring change—is necessarily going to break the bank. Whenever you have to pare down your project because of cost, you simply have to decide what your priorities are. It may be that relocating the tub is ultimately more important to you than having the particular style of tub you've had your heart set on. The point is that you should not assume plumbing and wiring changes are inevitable or that they are necessarily too expensive. When you get into the actual planning, you'll see the ways in which you can play around with variations that can utilize existing lines, are esthetically pleasing, and fit your budget. For more details on plumbing and wiring changes, see page 56.

Your Notebook

The first phase of your project is design and planning. Your single most important tool during this phase is an ordinary notebook. Ring binders are best. They are more expensive than spiral-bound notebooks, but you can move pages around simply and neatly, whereas with a spiral notebook you'll end up tearing pages out in one place and stuffing them into others. Buy a notebook now, and start to make some lists of things you like about bathroom designs—or, in fact, about any designs at all—and things you do not like. When you look through a magazine or brochure and see a picture of an appealing bathroom or of anything you'd like to use in your own bathroom, cut it out. Tape it in your notebook along with any comments you want to make about it. Organize your notes and photographs into categories that make the most sense to you. Some of those categories might be Fixtures (which you might subdivide even further into Tubs, Showers, Washbasins, Toilets), Vanities, Floors, Counter-Top Surfaces, and so forth.

Assessing Your Present Bathroom

While you're gathering your ideas about designs, styles, fixtures, and fittings, examine the bathroom you're already living with. Even though there are things you do not like about it, you may find certain elements that you want to retain or modify only slightly. Two essential tools will help you do this. The first is the Bathroom Survey, a two-page exercise that will help you assess your bathroom in the specific terms of light, space, storage, layout, and so on. You will use this information to determine your remodeling priorities and to help guide your new

design. The second tool is the Existing Plan, a two-dimensional floor plan of your bathroom as it is today. This plan will be the foundation for your new layouts. If you plan to hire a designer or general contractor to handle the whole job for you, you may imagine you can save some time by skipping the Bathroom Survey and the Existing Plan. However, anyone involved in remodeling your bathroom will need the information these two steps generate, and it's a lot less expensive to gather such information on your own than with a consultant by your side.

The unusual feature of this dramatic bathroom is the cedar-lined shower stall. Accented by brass trim and accessories, the cedar is also used for the walls and vanity. Because no other major colors have been added, the standard glass-enclosed shower stall becomes the room's focal point. See Chapter Two (pages 13–23) for more design ideas.

THE BATHROOM SURVEY

Whether you're planning to simply spruce up your bathroom or to rip it apart and start over again from scratch, the questions that follow will help you identify the problems you want to correct and the esthetic features you want to improve. It is impossible for you to give a wrong answer to any question here. If the Survey asks you to think about a problem, and you find yourself thinking about a solution instead, go ahead and note the ideas that occur to you. Obviously, the questions are by no means exhaustive. They should help you focus on particular areas of your bathroom and stimulate questions of your own.

1. General Considerations

Begin by standing in the doorway of your bathroom with your notebook and a pen or pencil. As you gaze about you, what do you see that you want to change most? Next? And then? Start a list in your notebook of all the major reasons you want to remodel your bathroom and all the most important changes you want to make. Then look at the more specific features of your bathroom, answer the questions for each section, and make whatever notes seem appropriate to you.

2. Overall Design

Do you like the way your bathroom looks? What do you like about it, and what do you dislike about it? Is it too bright? Too dark? Too messy? Too sterile? Do you think your bathroom is boring? Cold? Garish? Cramped? Old-fashioned? Too small? Somber? Spacious? As you list the design factors you like or dislike in your bathroom, note the particular elements—such as color, light, or design style—that you think contribute to the atmosphere you want to change.

3. Space, Traffic, and Layout

Is there enough space in your bathroom for the people and activities that must be accommodated? If not, why not? For instance, are too many people using a limited number of fixtures? Are secondary activities (such as laundry, exercise equipment, or pet supplies) taking up room you need for primary bathroom uses? Do you have enough counter space? Enough mirror area? Enough privacy? Does your bathroom door open into the room, blocking space you could otherwise use? List the most important bathroom space and traffic prob-

lems you can think of, and note the times and circumstances when they are worst.

4. Space and Storage

Do you have enough storage space in your bathroom? Is the space you do have laid out in a way that is useful for the needs of your household? Do bottles and boxes crowd the corners of your sink or counter top? Are toothbrushes strewn across the landscape? Towels stacked on the counter top and toilet tank? As you list the storage problems you confront in your bathroom, think about the ones that bother you most, as well as those you could eliminate without remodeling your bathroom at all—such as throwing away that broken hair dryer your cousin left last Christmas or assigning everyone a regular place for his or her own towels and toothbrush.

5. Heating

Is your bathroom warm enough? Is it too warm? Do you have any control over the heat in the room? If you are not presently satisfied with the heating system in your bathroom, what changes would you like to make?

6. Surfaces

What materials cover your walls, floor, and ceiling? What do you like about these materials? What do you dislike about them? Are they easy or hard to keep clean? Have they peeled? Chipped? Mildewed? Cracked? Fallen off? Are the colors satisfactory? Have the surfaces worn well? Would you want to use these same sorts of surface coverings again?

7. Fixtures and Fittings

In bathrooms "fixtures" generally refer to the washbasin, toilet, tub, shower, and bidet (if there is one present). "Fittings" generally mean the hardware on these fixtures—the faucets, handles, and visible pipe. As you look at the fixtures and fittings in your own bathroom, what do you like or dislike about them? Are they too old? Too modern? Too small? Too large? Broken beyond repair? Difficult to clean? Difficult to use? Are the colors wrong for your taste? Is there some fixture you would like that you do not have at present? Would you prefer a single faucet for mixing water temperatures where you now have two? Would you prefer two where you now have one? As you list your thoughts about your bathroom fix-

tures and fittings, consider each one individually, and note whether you want to replace it or not. If you do, how would the replacement differ from your present fixture?

8. Accessories and Hardware

Certain accessories are fairly standard in the modern American bathroom. Start with our list, and add any others you wish, to complete this section of your Bathroom Survey.

Mirror	Toothbrush holder
Towel bar	Toilet tissue holder
Towel hook	Facial tissue holder
Chair/stool	Paper towel holder
Magazine/book rack	Wastebasket
Soap dish	Laundry basket/hamper
Cup/glass holder	Scale
Robe/clothes hooks	Door handles
	Drawer pulls

Do you have the accessories you want? Are they conveniently located? Do you like the materials, colors, and design? Is your soap dish deep enough? Is your towel bar wide enough? Can you see yourself in your mirror? Do you have enough space for your hand-washed laundry? Note any additions and subtractions you would like to make.

9. Lighting and Electrical Outlets

Do you like the lighting in your bathroom? Is there enough? Too much? What direction does your bathroom window face? When do you get the most natural light? Do you like the artificial light you have? Do you have incandescent or fluorescent light bulbs? Is the light too harsh? Too soft? Does it shine where you really need it? Do you like your lighting fixtures? Are there enough electrical outlets in your bathroom for your needs? Where are your outlets located? What do you use them for? Are they convenient? What electrical fixtures are permanently installed in your bathroom (heaters, ventilator fans, etc.)? Are you satisfied with their locations? Are you satisfied with the way they function? If not, what changes would you like to make?

10. Special Needs

Are there people in your household who have special needs, such as children or handicapped or elderly adults? What are their special needs? Does your present bathroom meet those needs? Can children reach the faucets? Can small children be bathed without discomfort for the responsible adult? Is the bathroom door wide enough for a wheelchair? Is the sink low enough for a wheelchair? Is there somewhere to sit in the shower?

Because function is the basis for all design, listing the needs of those who use the bathroom is particularly important.

11. Luxuries

In or adjacent to your bathroom, have you any luxury fixtures such as a whirlpool bath, steam cabinet, hot tub, or sauna? Which do you have? Which would you like? If you want such luxury fixtures, where would you put them? How important are they to you, compared to other priorities?

Your Priorities List

Once your Survey is complete, summarize your notes for all eleven sections, and develop a list of priorities from your summary. For example, if you noted that too many people are trying to use the washbasin in the morning, one of your priorities may be to clear up the morning traffic jam. If you also noted that you don't like the color of your washbasin, another notation may be to replace it. Then you'll want to order these notes according to their importance to you. Your priorities list will be important any time you have to choose among numerous alternatives, such as colors, sizes, and styles of fixtures, use of storage space, or selection of special features. But if you are on any sort of budget at all, the list can save you from catastrophe. It will show you at a glance where you must spend, where you would like to use your extra money, and where you can use whatever reserves you have left over. Without such a list it is all too easy to be swayed by a spectacular new tub or wallpaper that you truly love but that makes the difference between having or not having something you need much more. The list is a guide you can prepare when you are your most informed and clear-headed self, for use when you have forgotten why you ever started planning things at all.

YOUR EXISTING PLAN

Your Existing Plan is an exact rendering of your bathroom as it is right now, translated from three dimensions to two. It will form the basis for all your design changes and will teach you the skill of visualizing three dimensions while working in two. To make your Existing Plan, you will need a few simple tools that you can purchase at any art supply, drug, or variety store.

Carpenter's rule. It is very important that your measurements are precise. For this reason you should use a metal tape; cloth measuring tapes tend to stretch and yield inaccurate readings. A good length is 16 feet: It is long enough to cover most rooms, but short enough to handle easily.

When measuring always write your measurements in inches, rather than feet and inches: 5 feet as 60 inches, 5 feet 2 inches as 62 inches, and so forth. This is the way professional consultants, contractors, and suppliers measure, and you will be able to communicate with them more easily if you follow their approach. You will also be less likely to cause confusion: The supplier who reads your handwritten 5'1" will not think you mean 511" if you have already translated your figures to 61".

A small straightedge or T-square

Soft pencils. Some people find it useful to have pencils in several colors, to create color codes for different elements.

Graph paper. You will be making an exact drawing of your present bathroom plan, and your measurements on paper should translate easily to the full-size, three-dimensional room. Architects commonly employ a ¼-inch scale (¼ inch = 1 foot) for whole-house projects; however, the smaller dimensions of the bathroom allow you to use a ½-inch scale (½ inch = 1 foot). In this larger scale, each square on your graph paper equals 6 inches of your bathroom, and two squares equal 1 foot. If yours is an especially small room, you might even use a 1-inch scale (1 inch = 1 foot) so that you can see your plan in greater detail.

Architect's scale. This is optional, but you'll find it speeds up many of your measuring tasks. It is a three-sided ruler that translates your real measurements (say, 9 feet) directly into several different scale measurements (2¼ inches in a ¼-inch scale) and back

Measuring Checklist

Overall Dimensions. You want to know the size of the room, so take your measurements as if there were no doors, windows, fixtures, or cabinets. Certain dimensions may be different in one spot from what they are in another: The ceiling will be lower where a soffit encloses a long light fixture, for example, and alcoves or protrusions will affect a wall's overall dimensions. It may help to make a rough sketch as you measure, and you might want to re-check some of your dimensions when you draw your Existing Plan.

	Length	Width
Floor	_____	_____
Ceiling	_____	_____

	Length	Height
North wall	_____	_____
East wall	_____	_____
South wall	_____	_____
West wall	_____	_____
Angled wall	_____	_____

Adjacent Space. Measure the space surrounding your bathroom: closets, hallways, bedrooms, other rooms. Include doors, windows, hall width, and closet length, depth, and height. You may decide you want to use some of this space in your remodeling project.

Fixtures. Note the length, width, depth, and height of each fixture currently in your bathroom:

Type of Fixture

Bathtub _____	Bidet _____
Shower stall _____	Whirlpool _____
Shower door _____	Steam cabinet _____
Washbasin _____	Other _____
Toilet _____	

Storage Units. Measure all the storage units now in use in your bathroom and in the areas immediately adjacent to it.

Type of Unit	Length or Width	Depth	Height	Depth of Shelves
Closet	_____	_____	_____	_____
Vanity cabinet	_____	_____	_____	_____
Counter top	_____	_____	_____	_____
Closed wall cabinet	_____	_____	_____	_____
Open shelving	_____	_____	_____	_____
Recessed cabinet	_____	_____	_____	_____
Recessed shelves	_____	_____	_____	_____
Recessed accessories	_____	_____	_____	_____

Doors and Windows. For all doors and windows, note on which wall each window or door is located, the type of window or door you have and measure the following:

_____	Height
_____	Width
_____	Distance from top to ceiling
_____	Distance from floor to windowsill
_____	Distance from sides to adjacent walls
_____	Width of trim or molding

When all your measurements are complete, draw your bathroom to scale.

again, freeing you from the onerous task of doing arithmetic or punching numbers into your pocket calculator.

Half-inch drafting tape. This tape is less sticky than masking tape and therefore less likely to tear your tracing paper, but masking or adhesive tape can be used.

Templates. Templates of bathroom elements (tubs, washbasins, toilets, and so on) are available at art supply stores. They're not essential, but you may want to try one out. Drawing around the appropriately sized cutouts is faster and easier than making your own templates.

Eraser

Tracing paper

Measuring Your Bathroom

When you have all your materials assembled, measure all the dimensions that will be important when you start to plan your new bathroom. If you already know that you will be getting rid of your current vanity, you don't need to measure it, but measure anything that you may

keep, however remote the possibility may be. Start with the overall dimensions and work down to the details. If you plan to expand your bathroom, include both the wall and the adjacent space you expect to annex. If the wall has a doorway, you can measure its thickness at the jamb, but do not include any moldings in your measurements. Use the chart as a guideline for measuring your bathroom's perimeter and elements.

How to Draw Your Existing Plan

When all your measuring is completed, translate those measurements into a scale drawing. Imagine that you can take the roof off your house, and you are looking down into your bathroom. What you see from this bird's-eye perspective is what you will represent in your Existing Plan drawing. You may have to do some additional measuring to plot the exact locations of the various elements relative to each other. Write the measurements clearly but inconspicuously, so they will not distract you when you start to work with the drawing. When your scale drawing is complete, you're ready to start creating a new bathroom design.

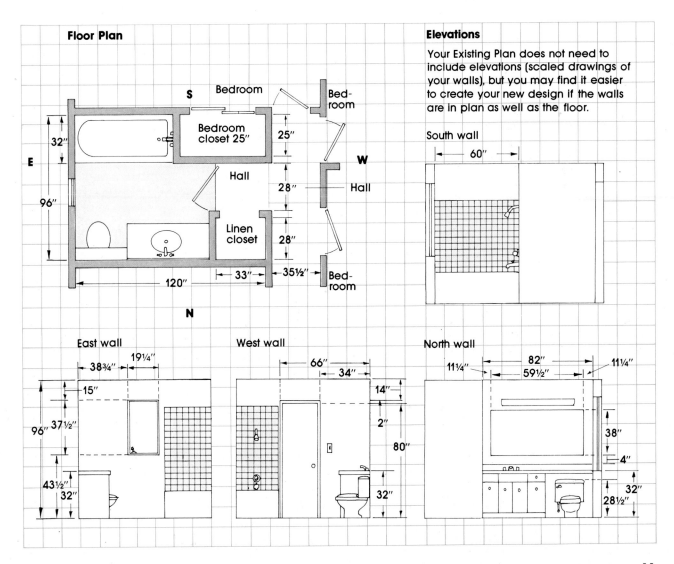

BATHROOM STYLES

Bathrooms come in all sizes, colors, and styles.
The same bathroom space can look dramatically
different depending on what elements you
choose and how you tie them together.
Take this photographic tour of bathrooms
to see what others have done.

When faced with design decisions, most people are concerned about coming up with good ideas, knowing how to put all the elements together in a pleasing way, and keeping within the budget. The purpose of this chapter and the next is to assist you with these issues of design.

Stages of Design

The design process is not mysterious. In fact, you've already begun. The first step is to establish your priorities, which you did in the Bathroom Survey; the next is to outline the givens of your current bathroom, which you did by drawing your Existing Plan. If you also have an idea of how much money you can spend and how much time you want to devote to the project, you've already got a good start. The remaining stages of design do not follow a rigid sequence; they overlap, merge into one another, and require that you flip back and forth among them. But the following list will assist you in the next stages of your new bathroom design.

1. Define the look or style you like and the elements that contribute to it. Look closely at the types of elements used in the bathrooms you like and at the way they are tied together visually.
2. Draw up alternative floor plans. Try out as many ideas as you can until you have a few promising finalists. If you're worried about budget, use these floor plans to get and compare some rough cost estimates.
3. Refine your design. Draw up elevations, or sketches of each wall. These sketches allow you to visualize your design and help you tie it together.

Style is very personal and need not adhere to rigid rules. Here, the rough-textured adobe counter and walls are combined with sleek, modern ceramic tiles, blinds, and basin fittings. Additional design features include an extension mirror, which permits the basin to be placed under the window, and a wall mirror that appears to double the open space.

4. Prepare a detailed cost estimate. If you plan to do the work yourself, estimate the cost of materials, tools, and supplies. If you intend to use professionals, get at least three bids.
5. Make a working drawing. This is the detailed drawing that will guide you or professionals through the physical work of remodeling and from which you will create your final materials list.
6. Establish a schedule of work. Plan the sequence of tasks, the approximate time each will take, who will do it, and when. Then write up contracts with any professionals you plan to hire.

When you've completed these steps, you'll be ready to translate your design into reality. Depending on your experience and interest, the time you take for each step will vary. Don't rush through. Many contractors say that the biggest problem with remodeling projects is poor planning. Even with the best construction techniques hasty planning can lead to disappointing results.

Define Your Style

There are no absolutes in "good" bathroom design. There are only pragmatic and esthetic questions, which boil down to: Is your design optimally functional, and do you like the way it looks?

Function is your basic building block: If the bathroom will be used by a number of people, for example, a good design will include a layout that eases traffic congestion and provides privacy and plenty of storage. If your bathroom does not meet your practical needs, the design is not "good."

A well-designed bathroom also highlights the best features of the room, and plays down those that are not especially pleasing. If the room is large and light and has an enormous panoramic view, a good designer will feature the window. On the other hand, if the room's window opens onto a dusty air shaft, it makes sense to obscure the view but not the light or ventilation.

From a different perspective, a good designer also creates an overall look or esthetic effect: A large bathroom might look spectacular with tall columns highlighted against dark wood walls and tiled floors. On the other hand, it might look equally compelling and dramatic if it had plain white fixtures and black accessories in a clean white shell. In this sense, design is very individual—it is a matter of style.

There is no right or wrong style. But it is important to know what your style is. Even when you are sketching basic floor plans—putting the tub here or the washbasin there—your design will go much more smoothly if you have a clear idea of the look and tone you are trying to achieve. Whether you realize it or not, you already have your own style. Whether you own a large house or a small condominium, you have made some decisions ·about the way your space is presented: You like dark colors or light ones, modern furnishings or antiques, simple or complex shapes. It may be that you like your style and don't want to change it; or you may want to try something new; or you may want to develop an entirely new sense of style. You can do any of these things as you design your bathroom.

First, look at the photos on the following pages. They represent a wide range of styles and ideas. Some may appeal to you immediately; others may leave you cold. They should serve as a starting point in defining your style. Then use your notebook. Take a close look at the photos you've been gathering. Compare them to those in this book. It may be that some photo comes close to the overall feeling you'd like to achieve in your own bathroom, or you may like only the knob on a cabinet. Whatever elements you like, make note of them.

Next, visit stores and showrooms where bathroom models are on display. In many of the salesrooms and showrooms you can pick up booklets and brochures showing a wide range of bathroom fixtures and other bathroom products, or the manufacturers may send such materials to you. You can use these picture- and information-laden guides to build your file of information about the ways in which different fixtures work and how readily available they are.

As you consider all your options, what appeals to you? Warm and cozy? Cool and sleek? Light and airy? Being clear about this will help you decide what elements you want to work with in your design. You'll also know what dimensions to use on your new plans—a Victorian tub generally takes up much less space than an elaborate whirlpool bath, for instance. In Chapter Three, you'll find charts that outline some of the basic sizes and features of common bathroom elements. You may want to keep these and your brochures handy when you get into full swing on your floor plans.

In addition to pinpointing the elements that contribute to the overall look you want to achieve, note how these elements are tied together—line, scale, shape, color, light, texture, and pattern. Sometimes you'll find that you like all the individual elements in a bathroom but don't like the room as a whole. It could be that you don't like the scale, or that you like white, but don't like shiny surfaces and strong lighting. Use all your photographs as tools for these kinds of clues to design. They will spark your own creativity.

Like the bathroom pictured on the cover, the one shown above is a light, open, indoor-outdoor room. Yet this bathroom has a distinctly different style. The high-contrast wallpaper, stark white vanity, and glossy floor finish all make a very strong statement. This effect is considerably softened, however, by the natural landscape, seen through the wall of glass and carried indoors with natural wood floors and trim. (A white floor

would have emphasized the bold design and created a sharp line of demarcation between inside and out instead of merging the two as the wood does.) The tub's placement against the window evokes a serene image of relaxing baths in a beautiful environment, and such a mental picture, although intangible, also counterbalances the room's bolder elements. The custom shower (reflected in the mirror) is snail-shaped, adding

an element of surprise to the room. Practical as well as pleasing, the snail shape eliminates the need for a shower door, but still offers total privacy. Reinforcing the light, open look of this bathroom are the glass corner shelves (left), which provide storage without totally covering the mirror. For another view of this bathroom, see page 68.

In many ways the bathroom shown on this page is very similar to the one pictured on pages 1 and 24. Both are about the same size, have almost identical layouts, and use a simple design. With its beige color, however, this bathroom immediately appears softer, and the art and pedestal basin both create a sculpted rather than structural look. Glass partitions between the shower, basin, and toilet separate the room's functions but do not interrupt its open feeling. These partitions also create a design theme that is continued in the framed mirror and, in a slightly altered form, in the holders above the basin. Chrome basin fittings (above) and towel holders (below) carry out the limited material scheme. Two other subtle but important details demonstrate how a design can be tied together: Extending the shower-seat line out into the room (below left) creates continuity between the two areas, and tiles around the base of the pedestal basin (above left) link it to the rest of the room.

In an old commercial building converted to residential use, this impressive bath area is an inexpensive solution to the problem of generous space. Defined by a line created with paint and carpet, the area is then filled with a plywood platform surrounding a standard tub. Simple lines, subtle colors, and sparing use of accessories all contribute to a feeling of elegant simplicity.

Dark colors and patterned wallpaper turn the limitation of a small space into the appeal of intimacy. Narrow ceiling-hung window blinds hide the standard shower next to the toilet, inexpensively separating the two areas. Track spotlights focus attention on the art while task lighting is supplied by a strip of bulbs above the mirror.

The spacious dressing area of the bathroom pictured on this page features hardwood floors, giving it a character quite distinct from that of the fully tiled shower and toilet room. When the mirrored pocket door is closed (bottom), you hardly know you're in a bathroom. A full wall of clothing and storage closets faces the vanity cabinets and drawers, and together these two units add up to an extraordinary amount of storage in a deceptively simple room. The white laminate counters, inset with recessed basins, carry out the crisp-edged style of the room. Makeup lights around the mirror provide task lighting, recessed ceiling lights provide the room's ambient light, and the skylight and corner window admit natural light without introducing an uninspiring outside view. The spare look of the room is deliberate; even the addition of a few small objects could dramatically alter this effect.

The bathroom on the facing page (also pictured on the back cover) is separated from the shower room by the custom-made storage unit (bottom left). Constructed of the same warm oak used in the bath, this storage unit repeats the shape of the wood-trimmed window near the bathtub, subtly linking the two areas. Glass shelves give it a light, delicate feeling, whereas wood shelves might have been too dark and bulky. The dual medicine cabinets (bottom right) provide two recessed storage units without interrupting the line of the mirror. As a practical consideration, the two basins and separate shower allow two or more people to use bathroom facilities at the same time. (For a discussion of other features in this bathroom, see page 2, "Back Cover.")

The owner of the bathroom shown above wanted to remodel without losing the original period feeling. The redwood walls give the room a clean modern look but also carry out the color of the antique medicine cabinet (right). Used on both the floor and shelf, the hexagonal mosaic tiles are new but mimic tiles of old. Behind the tub's end wall is a modern shower, finished with the same hexagonal tiles used on the floor. All the original fixtures remain, including the fittings on the tub and pedestal basin. The end result is a modern bathroom that effectively retains its original character.

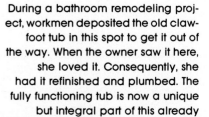

During a bathroom remodeling project, workmen deposited the old claw-foot tub in this spot to get it out of the way. When the owner saw it here, she loved it. Consequently, she had it refinished and plumbed. The fully functioning tub is now a unique but integral part of this already striking room.

As you enter the spacious bathroom shown on these two pages, a shower room is on your right and a vanity and toilet are on your left. Adjacent to the doorway, shelves and cabinets (above left) provide plenty of storage and serve as a privacy screen for the toilet. Brass fittings complement the 8-foot vanity (above right) that was once a turn-of-the-century shoe-store counter. Highlighting the beige and gold color scheme, are gold-finished mirror frames made from molding strips and both mirrors conceal recessed shelves. A 6-foot skylight moved from another part of the house, provides generous natural light over the vanity, contributing to the expansive, open quality of the room. Gold shower fittings (below left) give a touch of elegance to the handmade Mexican tiles in the shower, while the deck and shed roof (opposite page) bring the outdoor feeling inside. The one-way mirrored window, however, helps retain a sense of privacy.

DESIGNING YOUR NEW BATHROOM

This chapter shows you how to
create a floor plan that suits your needs
and how to use elevation sketches to tie your
design together. The Shopping Guide will help
you select fixtures and materials, and guidelines
for cost estimates and contracts will
help you complete your plans.

With ideas starting to pop, you'll want to get on with your sketches. During this phase, let your imagination go—changes in plumbing, wiring, heating, or structure may not be nearly as expensive or impossible as they might seem at first. As you get further into your planning, you'll develop a sense of what you can and cannot afford.

Plumbing and Wiring
You should know at the outset that you can move your washbasin a few inches to the right or left of its present position by using flexible supply lines, and in most situations you can move your tub, toilet, or basin up to 6 feet from the vent line without having to install all new plumbing (check local codes). As long as you have relatively easy access to your plumbing lines (through the basement or crawl space, perhaps) you can divert the lines to the new location without necessarily incurring a lot of extra expense.

These same principles hold true for your bathroom wiring. Changing a light fixture is a simple procedure. If you want to change the location of that fixture or add outlets where none exist now, you have to do more extensive work, but it is not necessarily expensive. Unless you're knowledgeable about wiring, you may want to go ahead and make your plans and then check with a professional.

Heating
If you already have a built-in heater operated by a wall switch or a pull chain, it probably works in conjunction with an exhaust fan set in your ceiling or wall. This sort of heater is simply an electrical fixture; it can be replaced with a higher quality model as long as your new heater does not place a greater demand on your wiring than the system can handle. Replacing the heater/fan is essentially the same as replacing the fan alone. If your bathroom has no built-in heating, the simplest solution is to purchase a separate space-heating unit. Electric space heaters are generally efficient in the small area of a bathroom, and installation is usually a matter of plugging the unit into an electrical outlet. If mounting is required, the heater will be packaged with specific instructions for doing the job.

Structural Changes
You can build recessed storage facilities, create privacy by erecting partitions, and sometimes even enlarge your bathroom by annexing adjacent space. There are many examples of this throughout the following pages.

Drawing the Plan
Tape tracing paper over your Existing Plan, and trace the shell of your bathroom, including walls, windows, and doorways. If you are considering expanding your bathroom into another room or into an adjacent closet, include that additional space on your tracing as well. Even if you don't have such plans at the moment, it's a good idea to include these surrounding spaces—you may change your mind about using them. If you're planning to keep any other elements, like the tub or toilet, include these on your drawing, too. Then, using a template or cutouts for the major elements in your bathroom, begin to play around with various floor plans.

Since you're not committed to any of your plans, take some chances with them. If some wonderful notion pops into your head when you're cooking, driving to work, or lounging in your tub, make a note of it and try it out. The great physicist, Albert Einstein, said he got some of his best ideas while shaving. Even if you're worried about cost, go ahead and sketch your idea. You may find ways to alter your most brilliant ideas to fit your budget, but you'll never know what those ideas are if you don't try them.

Set against the all-white tile background, the towel bar and exposed shower pipe become the featured elements of this shower stall, which is the other half of the bathroom shown on page 1. Note how even a small touch of color diminishes the intensity of this very structural design.

FLOOR PLANS

Ordering Your Ideas

As you draw, you may be flooded with new ideas, and there are some basic principles that will help keep you from being overwhelmed by this flood. The bathroom is generally a small space with a high concentration of use. The best treatments are the simple ones that employ continuous and harmonious lines, with accents of color and shape. When you're doing a floor plan, just think about the main areas of use at first—the washbasin, tub and shower, toilet, and counter space—and the traffic patterns to and from those areas. Think about who uses the bathroom and when, and try to arrange fixtures to limit congestion in one area. Then build other structural elements around these areas, creating adequate storage space where you need it and easy access to frequently used elements—mirrors, towel bars, light switches, and outlets. The first step in any plan is to establish a sound floor plan that functions well for whoever is using the space. Everything else will follow. If you focus on function at the outset, you won't go off in too many directions at once.

If you just want to change the look of your bathroom without making structural changes, you can start with your Existing Plan and draw new elevations: Sketch each wall head on, and play around with ideas for a new vanity, mirror, lights, surface coverings, and so on. Even superficial work on finish treatments may entirely satisfy your urge to remodel. You'll find guidelines for this part of your design on pages 32–37. If you want to make more substantial changes, you'll probably want to do a variety of floor plans first, establishing the more fundamental changes before you do elevation sketches. Take a look at the plans on the following pages. They illustrate ten variations of the single Existing Plan shown on page 10. These illustrations show you how much you can do with a single bathroom. Plan 1, for example, entails "cosmetic" changes only. The remodeling consists of upgrading finish treatments alone. The idea of remodeling does not necessarily mean everything old must go and only the new can be incorporated into your design. Be sure to look for ways to use what you have. There's no point in spending a lot of money when you can refurbish or enhance what is already there. For example, a pedestal washbasin may be inconvenient because it lacks surrounding counter space. But there may be ways to build shelf space above the basin or nearby and then feature this bathroom element. Every new bathroom need not have a basin embedded in a vanity.

Plan 2 leaves all the plumbing intact, but replaces the tub with a shower and shows yet a third cosmetic change. Plans 3–10 illustrate more substantial changes demonstrating how the same space can be totally altered to meet different needs or tastes. These sample plans should get you going and help you see new possibilities for your own bathroom. Check your brochures and the charts on pages 38–47 for dimensions of the various elements you want to use, and then follow this same process, creating as many plans as you want. You're likely to be surprised at what you can do with your old bathroom.

PLAN 1

The goal of this plan is to gain storage space and to give the bathroom a softer look. Note that none of the fixtures (tub, basin, toilet) are moved or changed, and the tile around the tub/shower combination is retained. By building a soffit on two walls to house lights, and over the tub to house the shower curtain, the beginning of an integrated look is achieved.

1. Exchange glass shower doors for softer feel of shower curtain. Wrap shower curtain around end of tub.
2. Build soffit rail across north and east walls to house recessed lights, and over tub edge to cover shower curtain rod. Creates a unified line around top of bathroom.
3. Build shelving over toilet back, with shelf uprights of same material as soffit holding glass shelves.
4. Exchange sheet vinyl for 12- by 12-inch ceramic tiles, with matte finish.
5. Hang medicine cabinet to left of washbasin. Edge with same material as soffit.
6. Exchange sliding glass mirror for slightly smaller full mirror wall.
7. Repaint vanity and add new hardware.
8. Potted plants cascade over soffits.
9. Window covered with same fabric as shower curtain.
10. New towel bars.

PLAN 2

Replacing the tub with a shower creates a second area for putting on makeup or shaving. Note, however, that the plumbing has not been changed—the shower wall is the same as it was before, although new lighting is required on the south wall.

1. Replace tub with shower.
2. Install vanity cabinet with storage above and below (see 12–14).
3. Synthetic marble counter top.
4. Lay carpet over existing floor.
5. Replace standard toilet with new low-line toilet.
6. Replace vanity with custom-built unit, including magazine racks on beveled portion.
7. Replace washbasin.
8. Install soffit full length of north wall.
9. Replace sliding mirror with single piece on full wall.
10. Install new towel bars.
11. Install soffit for lights over shower and new vanity.
12. Mirror facing on cabinet doors. Door opens from bottom. Cabinet stores linens.
13. Mirror on back wall.
14. Lower vanity has drawers for grooming items and lower cabinet with slide-out shelves for additional storage.
15. Glass shower door.

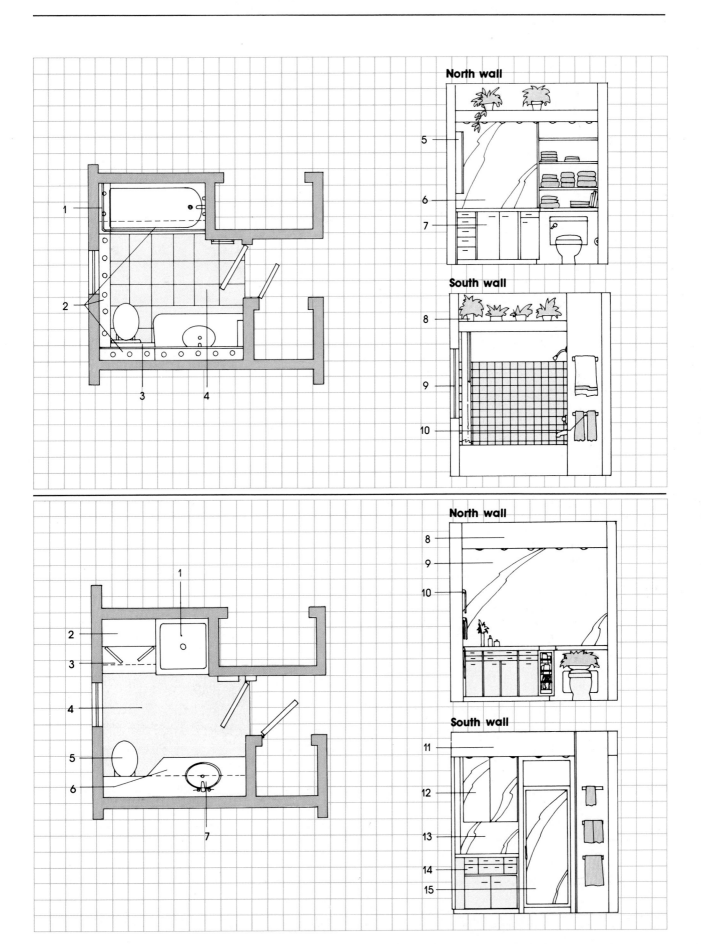

North wall

5

6

7

South wall

8

9

10

North wall

8

9

10

South wall

11

12

13

14

15

1

2

3

4

1

2

3

4

5

6

7

PLAN 3

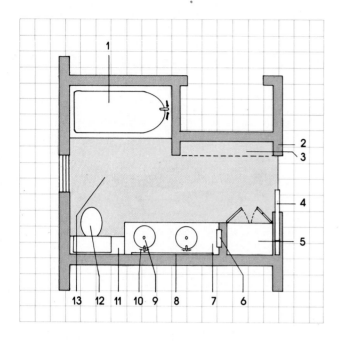

PLAN 4

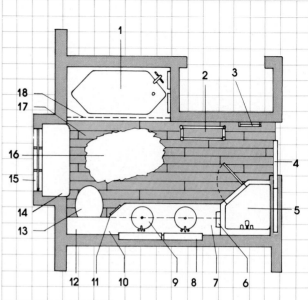

More storage and a second basin are the concerns in this plan. Because the hall closet is used almost exclusively for towels and linens, there is no reason why it can't be incorporated into the bathroom itself. Moving the bathroom door back to open directly from the hall makes the bathroom seem much larger. A pocket door eliminates traffic problems. Shifting the door slightly to the left as you enter the bath extends the wall on the other side, creating space for shallow, but useful, storage shelves. Flexible supply lines make the addition of a second basin relatively easy. Because the entire width of the closet is not used for new storage, it can be made narrower, which lengthens the vanity and counter top.

1. Current tub with new shower doors and fittings.
2. Extended wall creating space for storage—bathroom door moved out to hall and shifted to left.
3. 8-inch shelves—with bi-fold doors for storing bathroom and cleaning supplies.
4. Pocket door.
5. New storage unit—drawers below, doors above—narrower than old closet.
6. Recessed medicine cabinet.
7. Extended vanity to take up space left from closet.
8. Mirrored wall with indirect lighting in soffit above using existing wiring.
9. Two new basins, tapping lines for second basin.
10. New fittings for basin.
11. Cabinet above toilet back for additional storage.
12. Current toilet, with new seat and cover.
13. New vinyl floor.

In this variation the goal is to separate the tub and shower, add a second basin, and upgrade the overall look of the bathroom. Annexing the entire hall closet and replacing the swing-out door with a pocket door makes the bathroom seem significantly larger. The major plumbing change is the addition of the shower, which requires new supply lines and tapping into the existing drain and vent lines. Crawl space access makes this feasible. An optional but attractive feature is the window seat. It requires breaking out the outside wall, but adds an entirely new dimension to the bathroom.

1. New tub.
2. Freestanding storage shelves.
3. Towel bars.
4. Pocket door.
5. Corner shower in old closet space.
6. Towel bar.
7. Soffit with recessed lights over basins.
8. Recessed medicine cabinets.
9. New round basins.
10. New vanity with extension over toilet back, cultured marble counter top.
11. Magazine racks.
12. Shelves over toilet back.
13. New low-line toilet.
14. Window seat with storage below and recessed lighting above.
15. New, larger windows with louvered shutters.
16. Area rug.
17. Wood plank floor with polyurethane finish.
18. Dropped ceiling over tub.

PLAN 5

PLAN 6

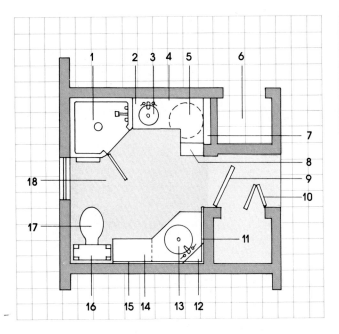

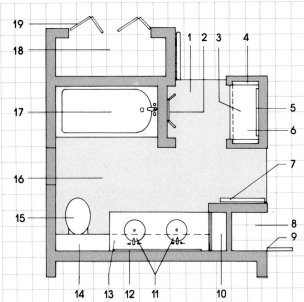

This plan provides two separate washing areas to clear up a traffic jam at the basin in the morning. By annexing part of the bedroom closet and replacing the tub with a shower, the design provides more space overall and two entirely separate basins and vanities. This is the first plan that requires significant movement in the plumbing, but it is not out of the question when the supply and drain lines are accessible from the crawl space under the house. Lighting over the second vanity requires some new wiring.

1. Tub replaced by shower on end wall—plumbing supply and drain lines rerouted from crawl space under house.
2. Custom-built corner vanity with drawers to left, storage beneath.
3. New round basin.
4. Mirror above vanity.
5. Lazy susan in corner of vanity for easy access.
6. Structural change to annex part of bedroom closet.
7. Recessed medicine cabinet in new wall.
8. Drawers in vanity.
9. Swing-out bathroom door.
10. Bi-fold linen closet door.
11. Mirror wall extends around corner.
12. Glass corner shelves.
13. New basin set at angle.
14. Custom-built vanity with slide-out shelves for maximum storage.
15. Mirrored wall.
16. Glass shelves above toilet back—in wood frame.
17. New toilet seat and cover.
18. New vinyl floor.

When adults and children share a bathroom, crowding at the mirror can be a problem. Annexing the bedroom closet and creating an entrance from the bedroom adds a separate dressing area for adults. In this case, a new closet is built out into the bedroom, because bathroom space is needed more. The hall closet is divided and the door changed to open into the hall. Note that there are virtually no plumbing changes in this plan—the addition of a second basin is easy and inexpensive.

1. Entire closet annexed for new dressing area.
2. Full-length three-way mirror.
3. Bureau with drawers for storage below.
4. Recessed shelves built in for cosmetics and so on.
5. Mirror back.
6. Overhead lighting in soffit or on track.
7. Bathroom door opening directly from main hall.
8. Hall linen closet divided, with shallower shelves giving easier access.
9. Closet door opening directly onto main hall.
10. Shelves for towel storage, with access directly from bathroom.
11. Two new basins—new vanity and counter top.
12. Large mirror affixed directly to wall.
13. Overhead lighting in soffit or on track.
14. Storage shelves over toilet back.
15. Same toilet with new seat and lid.
16. New sheet vinyl floor.
17. Same tub with new fittings and shower door.
18. New closet built out into bedroom—longer than old closet.
19. Bi-fold doors giving easier access to entire closet space.

PLAN 7

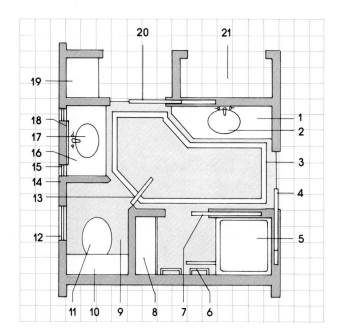

PLAN 8

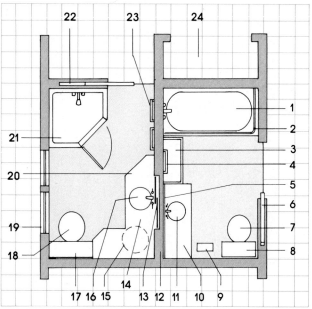

When there is only one bathroom for the family, several people can use the space at the same time if there is enough privacy. In this plan, the bedroom closet space is annexed to create space for a new vanity area. By moving the existing basin and vanity and annexing the hall closet, the bathroom has room for a fully enclosed shower and dressing area. Removing the tub makes space for a second vanity area and access from the bedroom, which limits traffic jams. The toilet is also fully enclosed for additional privacy. You could also add a skylight over the central space.

1. Old closet replaced by new vanity designed for maximum storage—pull-out shelves, drawers.
2. New basin and fittings—plumbing lines diverted from old tub.
3. New flooring with narrow contrasting band to emphasize new shape.
4. Pocket door opening directly from main hall.
5. Shower installed in place of hall closet.
6. Towel bars.
7. Enclosure for shower room with pocket door.
8. Bench with storage drawers below for towels.
9. Dropped ceiling with recessed lighting for enclosed toilet and shower room.
10. Cabinet for storage above toilet back.
11. New toilet or toilet seat and cover.
12. Existing window moved to left—or new window.
13. Swing-out door for enclosed toilet.
14. Floor-to-ceiling partition to enclose toilet for privacy.
15. New narrow windows on either side of vanity.
16. New vanity designed for maximum storage.
17. New basin—plumbing lines diverted from old tub.
18. Mirror above vanity.
19. Built-in dresser drawers with mirror above.
20. New entrance from bedroom with pocket door.
21. New closet in bedroom space.

If one bathroom is just not enough despite privacy features, it is possible to divide this same space into two small but functional bathrooms by using both closets. One bathroom has a shower; the other a 54-inch tub. A skylight could be added to the inside bathroom, giving natural light and a feeling of space.

1. 54-inch tub in place of bedroom closet, using current shower diverter.
2. Wrap-around shower curtain.
3. Low bench with storage drawers below.
4. Towel bar.
5. Mirror above vanity.
6. Pocket door from hall.
7. New toilet—possibly smaller than standard size.
8. Storage shelves above toilet back.
9. Stool for use by small children.
10. New vanity.
11. New basin and fittings.
12. New wall incorporating plumbing lines for both basins.
13. Recessed medicine cabinet for adult bath.
14. Custom-built vanity using all corner space.
15. Lazy susan in corner of vanity to increase access to space.
16. New basin.
17. Storage unit above toilet back—open shelves or closed cabinet.
18. Same toilet with new seat and cover.
19. Old window replaced by two new ones.
20. Open angled shelves at end of vanity.
21. New shower unit.
22. Pocket door between bath and bedroom.
23. Towel bars.
24. New closet in bedroom space.

PLAN 9

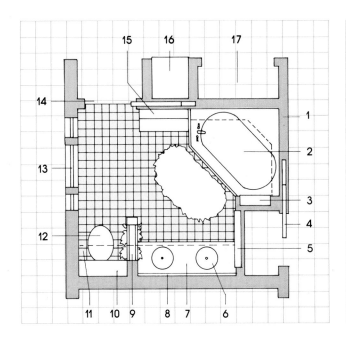

PLAN 10

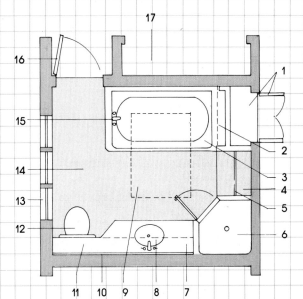

It could be that access to the bathroom from the hall is not necessary. Perhaps there is another bath for family members or guests. In that case, you have the option of turning this into a luxury bathroom accessible only through the master bedroom. By using all of the bedroom closet, you can retain linen storage accessible from the hall and create space for a sumptuous corner tub. This plan calls for the tub to be built in, but it could just as easily be a Victorian clawfoot or a sunken tub.

1. Wall enclosing old entry to bathroom.
2. Whirlpool tub at angle, using old plumbing and replacing existing closet.
3. Built-in shelves for storage of tub items.
4. Pocket door for altered linen closet.
5. Recessed medicine cabinet built into back of closet wall.
6. New basins.
7. New vanity with drawers and pull-out shelves.
8. Large mirror on wall.
9. Half-wall divider between toilet and vanity for some privacy.
10. Cabinet above toilet back with drawers below and enclosed shelves above.
11. Soffit with recessed lights on full length of north wall.
12. New toilet in same location.
13. Single narrow window replaced by three windows extending from just above floor to soffit above—possibly sliding glass doors for access to patio or hot tub.
14. Pocket door between bedroom and bath.
15. Linen cabinet to soffit line—shallow shelves above, deeper ones below.
16. Built-in dresser drawers with mirror above.
17. New closet extending into bedroom space.

As your children grow up, your needs change. Two basins may no longer be necessary, and instead of maximum efficiency you may want a room that is spacious and relaxing. Plan 10 is another variation of a private bath accessible only from the bedroom. The separate tub and shower allow a relaxing soak or a quick rinse. Even if you remove the hall closet, you can retain hall storage just by shifting the enclosures around: Take out the bedroom closet, using part of it for the bathroom and the rest for cleaning supplies accessible from the hall. Plumbing changes are relatively minor in this plan, and you can focus on the materials and products that will give it the look and feel you want.

1. Utility closet with two louvered doors—created by annexing existing bedroom closet.
2. Soffit with recessed light above end and wall side of tub.
3. Whirlpool tub.
4. Built-in cabinet for towel and linen storage.
5. Cushioned seat—soffit with recessed lighting above.
6. Corner shower with pan and tiled walls—recessed light and moisture vent in ceiling.
7. New vanity in same location as old.
8. New basin and fittings in same location as old.
9. Skylight over central space and tub for lots of light.
10. Mirror extending entire length of wall.
11. Overhead lighting hidden behind soffit fascia board.
12. New low-line toilet.
13. Small narrow window replaced by large wall windows or doors leading to patio or hot tub.
14. New flooring—large tiles or carpet.
15. New fittings for tub—outside of tub enclosed with tile or wood.
16. New entrance to bathroom with hinged door.
17. Enlarged closet in bedroom space.

REFINE YOUR DESIGN

Spread out all your satisfactory floor plans and pick the ones you feel work the best—the "finalists" so to speak. Try combining the best elements in each one and see if you can come up with an even better plan. You may try this several times before settling on the arrangement of your bathroom that serves most of your practical needs and has the best feeling to it.

Check Your Layout Against Reality

Before you move on, make sure your layout will actually work. If you place fixtures and other large units of furniture too close together, you cannot expect the room to be either comfortable or functional. In most parts of the country plumbing codes determine the legal clearance space around fixtures. But the codes vary from one locale to the next, and the standards they set are minimums, not ideals. Consult your local codes and experiment with the minimum requirements for your region. Have a friend or a family member stand 18 inches away from the shower door and find out what it feels like to step out into that restricted a space; measure to find out if 18 inches will really be adequate knee space in front of the toilet; try to wash your face with only 14 inches between the center of your sink and the side wall. These are some of the legal minimums specified by some codes in the United States. Since you're already going to the trouble and expense of redoing your bathroom to suit yourself and your family, you may want something more.

Esthetic Considerations

Once you feel satisfied that your basic layout meets your needs, move on to the more esthetic design considerations. When you start to make esthetic choices about remodeling your bathroom, there are no hard and fast rules. Some people establish a color preference first and work other elements into the scheme; others prefer to select their fixtures first. If you have some special feature in mind—perhaps you're installing an antique pull-chain toilet you just bought—choose other items which support the tone of this element.

The way you approach the esthetic considerations is up to you, but continue planning as if it were a game. You might think of it as a picture puzzle; you are trying to develop a completed picture of your bathroom by assembling pieces that really fit. There is bound to be a certain amount of trial and error, so bear in mind that each idea—even those you end up discarding—contributes to the final effect.

Visualizing Your Design

Part of the confusion that arises at this stage of bathroom planning results from the difficulty most people have in visualizing how their floor plans will translate into three-dimensional reality. One way to deal with this is to draw elevations. You may know that you want a cabinet over the toilet back, but how wide will it be and how tall? Do you want open shelves or doors covering them? How far above the tank do you want it to start? How does it tie in with the rest of the elements on the wall? What

Elevations

These elevation sketches of plan 10 on page 31 show you how a design is tied together with line, shape, and scale.

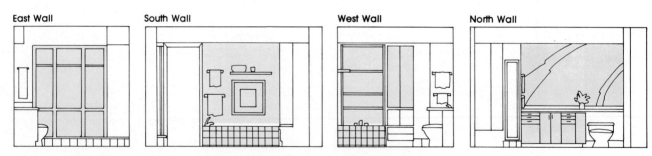

East Wall · South Wall · West Wall · North Wall

Large scale elements are used to keep the size of the room integrated as a whole.

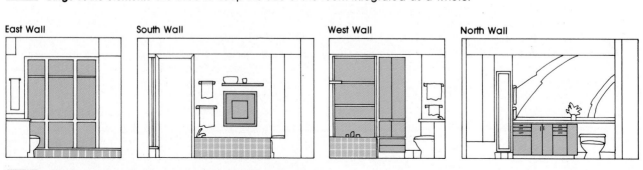

East Wall · South Wall · West Wall · North Wall

Small scale elements carry out the large-scale effect.

kinds of materials do you want to use? You can settle these questions with an elevation sketch.

Drawing Elevations

If you approach your elevation sketches first with an eye to line, scale, and shape and then focus on color, light, and materials, you can avoid feeling confused by too many choices at once. Break them down, deal with one or two principles at a time, and your ideas will fall into place. The sketches below are elevations of Plan 10, shown on page 31. They should give you some idea how to approach your own elevation sketches.

Line

Horizontals—created in obvious ways by tile borders or painted trim or in more subtle ways by the tops of doors and windows, soffits, counters, and floors—carry the same or harmonious line around the room and hold the space steady. Use these lines to create continuity. For example, if you have a wall 6 feet wide and can afford the space, use a 6-foot vanity to carry the line through the horizontal space instead of chopping it up with a 4-foot vanity. If you're deciding how high to make a wall cabinet, consider tying it in with the tops of doors and windows even if the top shelf will be impossible to reach. Here your consideration is the overall effect of your design rather than pure function. Finish treatments, like ceiling moldings and light soffits, can also be used to unify the lines in your bathroom. When you bring tile only part way up the wall, you create another horizontal line. It doesn't have to be arbitrary. Instead, you can tie it

in with other elements and carry it around the room. The idea is to be aware of these obvious and not-so-obvious lines and use them to your advantage.

Scale

Small spaces often use dropped ceilings to proportion the volume of the room. Unless you specifically choose to feature a high ceiling even in a small room, you want to avoid a vertical tunnel effect. By the same token, if you're installing a skylight in a high ceiling, you want it big enough so it doesn't feel like a suction cup.

If your bathroom space is small, you may want to avoid large, closed cabinets. You can change the apparent bulk of a shelving unit by using open shelves on the wall or perhaps even in one part of your vanity. Enlarging or pushing out a window changes the apparent volume of the whole room, so when you're sketching elevations, try altering the size and type of your windows. Considering the volume of your bathroom allows you to scale its elements appropriately.

Shape

Continuity in shape also lends harmony to your design. If you have narrow vertical shelving units, a single oval mirror, round basins, and wide rectangular counter surfaces, you may feel jangled by your design. Obviously this doesn't mean everything has to be the same shape, but try to avoid too many contrasting shapes; rather, try to tie the whole together by using similar, repeated shapes. Look at the elevation sketches in this chapter with this principle in mind.

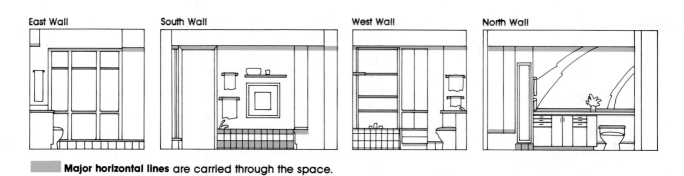

East Wall **South Wall** **West Wall** **North Wall**

 Major horizontal lines are carried through the space.

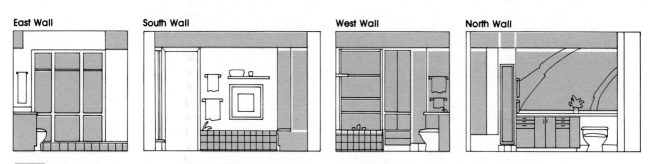

East Wall **South Wall** **West Wall** **North Wall**

 Shape. Square, rectangular, and elongated rectangular shapes are repeated throughout the room.

COLOR & LIGHT

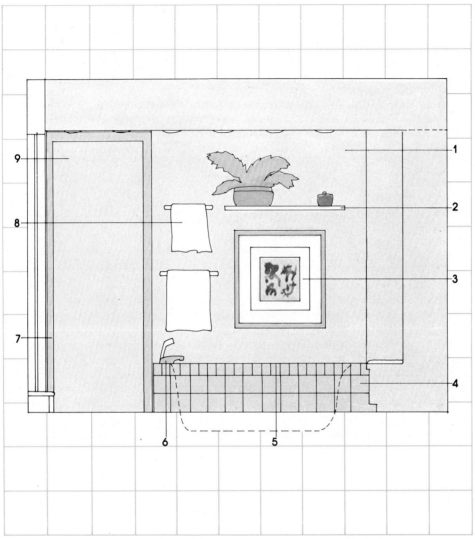

South wall

1 Light apricot for all major vertical surfaces.
2 White shelf.
3 Oriental print with thin slate frame and wide white matte.
4 Light gray tiles with slate gray grout.
5 White tub.
6 Chrome and white ceramic fittings.
7 Slightly darker shade of apricot for trim and molding.
8 White towels and towel bars.
9 Door painted in same light apricot used on walls.

Color is often your first impression of a room, and it is usually the impression that lasts the longest. Its impact can overshadow the shape, texture, and arrangement of objects, and can actually make fixtures and even whole rooms appear to change size. Because a bathroom contains a variety of very different components—wall and floor surfaces, fixtures, furnishings, and accessories—the range of effects you can create with color is virtually limitless.

Warm and cool colors. Colors may be seen as cool or warm. Those closest to blue tend to feel cool; those closest to red tend to feel warm. A cool color appears to make surfaces and objects recede, and warm colors appear to make surfaces and objects advance. As a result, a cool-colored room may seem larger than it is and a warm-colored room may seem smaller. The feel of colors in the middle ranges depends largely on how much blue or yellow they contain. Blues and greens with a lot of yellow can appear warm, and reds or yellows with a great deal of blue in them will seem cooler. Even whites, grays, browns, and blacks can appear either cool or warm depending on the amount of yellow or

blue they contain. If you know that you want a warm, cozy bathroom, you can use this basic principle to guide your choice of basic color families. Colors chosen from within the same family tend to produce a soothing effect, whereas combining colors from the opposite sides of the color wheel—red/green, blue/orange, yellow/purple—tend to make a strong impression.

Color schemes. Selecting basic color families is a very personal choice. You don't have to know why you like certain colors—if you like them, use them. But use them well. Start by choosing a color scheme—you can begin with your fixtures or any other element and build from there. If you consider your floor material as a base, other horizontal planes tend to look best when they're the same or in a close family. Fixtures (basins, tubs, and toilets) can provide contrast. Most color schemes fall into one of three categories:

In the *monochromatic* scheme, a single color in varying degrees of tone and value is used for all major surfaces and fixtures. The effect can be one of peace and security. Accessories are chosen in related or complementary accent colors.

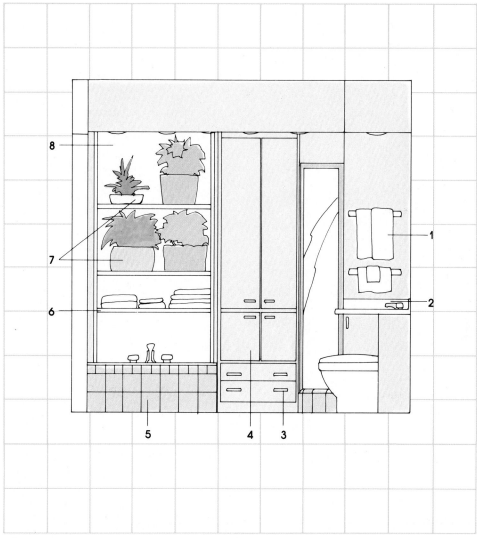

West Wall

1 White towels.
2 White counter top.
3 White drawer pulls.
4 Storage unit in same light apricot used on walls.
5 Light gray tile with slate gray grout encloses tub sides and ledge.
6 White shelves.
7 White and apricot pottery plus natural baskets to hold plants.
8 White wall behind shelves.

In the *complementary* scheme, contrasting colors are used on major surfaces and for fixtures. Properly realized, this scheme produces excitement and vivacity; but if it gets out of hand, which it frequently does, a sort of manic confusion can result. For the person who wants to employ a complementary color scheme but feels uncertain about the way to achieve a pleasing result, a reasonably safe solution is to choose one dominant color for major areas like walls, floors, and ceilings, and one supporting color for trim, woodwork, and accents.

The *related* color scheme is created by using colors connected by a common base. Yellow might be used with yellow-green and green, or with yellow-orange and orange. Accessories in different hues of the related colors can blend or provide contrast.

Color and space. These two elements work together. If you're trying to make a large bathroom look smaller, you can use more intense colors. Conversely, you can make a small room look larger by using more diffuse and softer colors. Or you can make a large room look even bigger or a small room even cozier. Either way, you can consciously use this principle of light and space

to create the desired effect. You can also make your bathroom seem to change shape: Darker floors and vertical surfaces coupled with a light ceiling make it seem taller. A dark ceiling with light walls, cabinets, and floors will make it seem wider and lower. Darker colors at the end of the room will shorten its visual length. There is a limit to what you can do with this principle, but it can guide some of your choices.

Color and light. Any color will look different in bright sunshine and under fluorescent tubes. When selecting paint, fixtures, or flooring, choose your colors by examining them in your own bathroom. You may be in for a big surprise when something you were sure was green looks blue, or when something you knew was red looks orange. Examining a color in your own home will save you a lot of disappointments. Try not to order a colored fixture from a catalog. The way in which the photographed piece was lit, the quality of the printing, and the conditions under which you are viewing the picture, can all combine to give you an erroneous sense of the true color. Instead, once you have decided on a color, see the fixture itself or another of the same color.

LIGHT, PATTERN, & TEXTURE

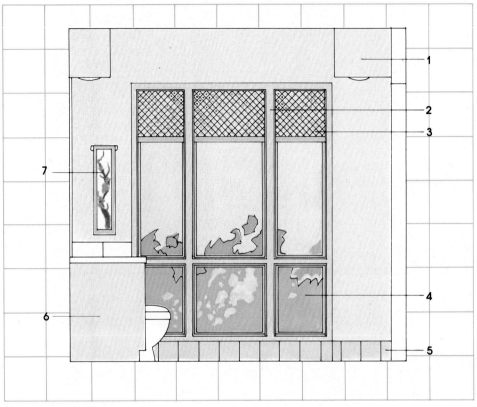

East Wall

1. Light apricot for all major vertical surfaces.
2. Slightly darker shade of apricot for trim and molding.
3. Fabric shades with a small, grid-like print: light apricot background, gray lines, light turquoise dot.
4. Natural greenery.
5. Light gray tile with slate gray grout.
6. Vanity painted in same light apricot used on walls.
7. Oriental print.

Natural light. If your bathroom windows face north or east, the natural light will be cool. Cool colors will feel extremely cold in such light, and dull colors will seem even duller. Unless these are the effects you want to achieve, plan your bathroom's decor with warm colors in mind to offset the effects of the room's natural light. On the other hand, windows facing south and west provide warm light, which makes warm colors feel very hot, and bright colors appear intense. Unless you want your bathroom to radiate a sort of concentrated heat, you will want to design the room with cooler colors.

If you are uncertain about the quality of the natural light your bathroom receives, look at the room early in the morning, at about noon, sometime in the middle of the day, and again toward evening. When is the light brightest? Softest? Most important, when do you like it best? Try to achieve that quality of light by selecting colors that support it. If you want more natural light, you can enlarge existing windows or, if your bathroom is on the top floor, add a skylight. These types of changes can, but need not, be costly, and they're certainly worth considering if light is a problem in your bathroom. You can also install a large reflecting surface on the wall opposite or adjacent to your window. This can nearly double the effective daylight in your bathroom.

Artificial light. There will be some occasions when you need light that nature does not provide. Artificial light has no less impact on color than natural light has although its effects are different. Normal *incandescent* lighting is warm, particularly if it is bright; it tends to harmonize and blend colors. Its effects are generally flattering and relaxing. When incandescent lighting is dim, colors lose many of their highlights. They darken and dull. This is why the "romantic" effects of dimly lit restaurants are punctuated by the localized brightness of table lamps. In the same fashion, if you are using a low-level incandescent general light, you should plan to provide other sorts of brighter lighting in specific areas.

The three principal kinds of *fluorescent* lights are cool white, warm white, and deluxe warm white. Cool white is the most commonly used, and is the one that tinges everything vaguely blue. Warm white casts an obscurely unhealthy yellow pall. But deluxe warm white comes closest to producing a stable, realistic, useful light, and is the one most often recommended by professionals using fluorescent lighting. Fluorescent lights radiate less heat and are less expensive to operate, but use them cautiously to achieve particular effects.

Planning Your Lighting

Because of the many varied activities that take place in the bathroom, it is impossible to overplan your lighting in this room. If you shave or make up in the bathroom, you need a light that is placed to shine on your face—not on the mirror—without throwing odd shadows. Light fixtures are often placed on the ceiling because they are out of the way and because from that height they cast light over the largest possible bathroom area. But track lights, lamps, and wall sconces lend themselves to the specific needs in a bathroom.

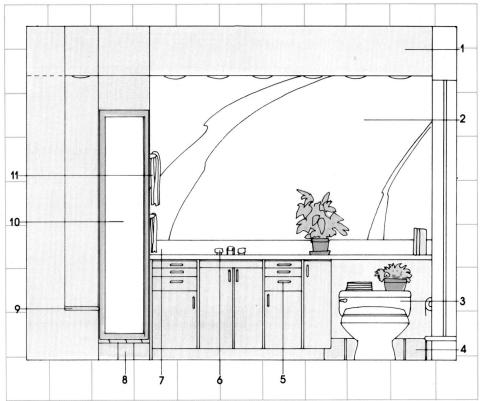

North Wall

1 Same light apricot used on soffit.
2 Full-wall mirror.
3 White toilet.
4 Light gray tiles with slate gray grout carried around base of wall.
5 White ceramic drawer pulls.
6 White ceramic fittings for washbasin.
7 White counter top, backsplash, and basin.
8 Light gray tiles at floor level and in shower.
9 Cushion covered in same fabric as roman shades.
10 Clear glass shower door.
11 White towels.

In the past decade or so, a highly useful lighting concept, know as task/ambient lighting, has been making its way out of the office environment and into the home. It refers to a two-part lighting arrangement with task lights specifically directed to work areas and ambient lights providing general room illumination. Whether you use an overhead fixture, track lights, or soffit lights hidden behind a lowered portion of the ceiling, ambient light permits the use of inexpensive, low-wattage, indirect illumination for general activities. Add specific, direct task lighting, and you have an attractive and efficient system that reduces eye fatigue and offers varied effects for different occasions or times of day.

Pattern

If your bathroom is small, take special care when selecting patterned wallpaper, fabric, or floor surfaces. Large-scale patterns containing more than three colors can overpower a small room. If you want lots of colors in your pattern, the smaller prints will probably work better. If you want a large print, you're likely to do better with only one or two colors, which can be bold by virtue of contrast rather than loud by being busy with colors. Be aware that even tiles can add pattern to a room. Something as minor as grout lines can create a noticeable visual effect—whereas white tile and white grout give the impression of a continuous, plain surface, grout that contrasts with the tiles, such as blue tile with white grout or light gray tiles with slate gray grout, punctuates the pattern. Simplicity is always a helpful guide.

Texture

The basic principle governing use of texture in the bathroom is much the same as for other design elements—don't overdo it. If you want a warm, cozy feeling, you'll want carpets or rugs, thick terry towels, the "textures" of displayed items on open shelves, and soft, matte finishes. If you want a sleek look, use smooth surfaces with a high gloss and crisp edges, such as mirrors and glass. Be aware that patterns create visual textures, so go easy with them. You can really see the effects of texture when you focus on only one color. Even a "cold," all-white room can take on a soft character if it contains various textures such as soft, matte walls, terry towels, a woven throw rug, a fabric shade, and a few etched accent tiles.

Detail: Accessories and Hardware

The smallest appointments can complete a bathroom design, or undo it. A single bright tile set in a quiet wall creates a major esthetic effect. Coordinating details is not difficult if you plan ahead. Knowing you will have a lot of wood surfaces might inspire you to use shiny brass hardware and hooks; in a bright white room with white fixtures, you might prefer polished chrome, stainless steel, mirror, and lucite. Fittings on the tub and basin certainly ought to be related, but when you've gone that far, why forget to match the toilet handle? Door and drawer pulls, hinges and hooks, towels and flowers, sponges and soaps, and even the toothbrush and toilet paper holders can be given the same attention lavished on walls and fixtures.

SHOPPING GUIDE

Shopping for the various elements in your bathroom will introduce you to an amazing variety of products and materials. The charts on the following pages are designed to categorize some of the variables and help you make your selections. The charts are by no means exhaustive; for every generality there is an exception. But by perusing these charts you can prepare yourself with some basic information and simplify your shopping.

Vanity Cabinets

Vanities are offered in many styles and materials, and are made with a variety of construction techniques. You can purchase the vanity base as a separate unit and then buy a counter top and basin of your choice, or you can obtain the counter top as part of the whole package. In this case, the basin is molded into the counter top and the entire piece is usually made of cultured marble. The vanity styles most commonly available are illustrated here, but remember that you can always have custom cabinets built to your specifications in any style or material you like, or you can adapt a piece of furniture to hold a basin (see photograph on page 22). Aside from style, you should look for quality construction. Guidelines for quality are outlined here.

Vanity Construction Techniques

Cabinet Part		Look for . . .
Joints	Case parts (sides, bottom and back)	. . . solidly anchored corner braces. Most case parts are joined with glue and nails or screws. The corner braces ensure stability.
	Drawers	. . . joints that are dovetailed or made of some other interlocking construction. However, glue and nails are the most common—these should feel solid and secure.
	Doors and face frames	. . . doweled, mortise and tenon, tongue-in-groove or other interlocking joints, although some are constructed with glue and screws. Joints should feel solid and secure.
Door and drawer fronts		. . . solid material or at least a substantial feeling throughout, and finished edges. Make sure drawer face is securely joined to the sides (see comments on drawer joints above).
Drawer slides		. . . sturdy slides solidly attached to vanity cabinet with screws. Metal slides are the most common, but some wooden ones work well. Two side slides are generally better than a single, center one. Drawers should slide easily.
Hinges		. . . solidly attached hinges that feel secure. Some hinges are self-closing.
Catches		. . . ease in opening and closing doors. You shouldn't have to yank the door to get it open.

Vanity Styles

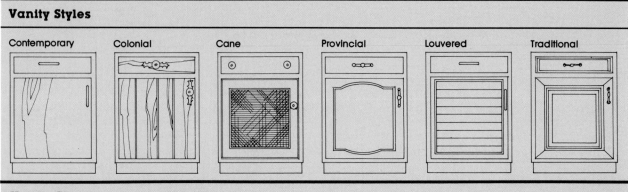

Contemporary   Colonial   Cane   Provincial   Louvered   Traditional

Vanity Sizes

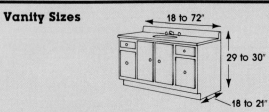

18 to 72"

29 to 30"

18 to 21"

Cabinet widths start at 18 inches and continue in 6-inch increments all the way up to 72 inches. Standard front-to-back depth is 18 to 21 inches, and standard height is 29 to 30 inches. One basin will fit in an 18-inch vanity, and two basins will fit comfortably in a vanity 48 to 72 inches wide.

Vanity Materials

Cabinet Part	Materials	Comments
Case parts (sides, bottom, and back)	Chipboard (also called particle-board)	Chipboard is commonly used for all case parts or as a filler between wood veneers. It should be thoroughly treated with sealant to prevent it from absorbing moisture, which can cause swelling.
	Plywood	Plywood is stronger than chipboard and gives the appearance of higher quality. More expensive than chipboard.
Face materials (face frame, drawer and door fronts)	Wood (oak, maple, birch, poplar, etc.)	"Solid wood" vanities generally mean that both lumber and high-quality plywood are used to construct face materials. In some instances the frame and fronts may be made of solid lumber.
	Plastic laminate	Plastic laminate comes in many colors and is easy to clean. The material should be solidly laminated to its base, which is commonly made of chipboard. Edges should be laminated or they can fracture and crumble. Usually less expensive than solid wood.
	Plastic styrene	Styrene is made to look like wood and is often advertised as having a hand-rubbed finish, but it is a plastic material. It is impervious to water and stains, easy to clean, and relatively inexpensive, but is also very lightweight.
	Chipboard veneered with vinyl or wood	Used for door and drawer fronts. Edges should also be veneered or they can fracture and crumble. Inexpensive.

Counter Tops

Counter tops can be made from a variety of materials with a broad range of colors, textures, and esthetic possibilities. If you want a molded basin, the counter-top materials available to you consist primarily of cultured (synthetic) marble. Vitreous china is also available, but on a more limited basis. If you want a washbasin set into a counter top, your choice of materials expands to include plastic laminate, ceramic tile, and treated wood.

Type	Comments
Cultured or synthetic marble	Generally comes only with basin already molded. Many variations on basin/counter-top configurations. Material is heavy, easy to clean, and comes in many pastel colors. Easy to install and relatively low in cost. Some cultured or synthetic marbles, such as Corian®, are also available in sheets, which you can use to make your own counter top for an inset washbasin. This material can be worked with standard woodworking tools with carbide blades. It is more expensive than other cultured marbles but has an elegant look, is very durable, and stains, scratches, or burns can be removed with a light sanding.
Vitreous china	Comes with basin already molded and in many colors. It is easy to clean and install and is less expensive than cultured marble, but it is not as readily available. The widest counter available is 36 inches.
Plastic laminate	Available in a vast range of colors, textures, and patterns at a relatively low price. Easy to clean, though it is subject to scorch and scratch marks. Laminating the plastic to the chipboard or plywood base and cutting the basin hole can be done by a professional. Cost for this service is moderate.
Ceramic tile	Tile counter tops require a plywood or cementboard base cut into the shape and size you want. This can be done fairly easily by a do-it-yourselfer. For details on tiles, see page 46.
Treated wood	For use in the bathroom, wood should be treated with a waterproofing substance like polyurethane. Prelaminated butcherblock is available in 25-inch widths and is sold by the running foot. Commonly used woods are oak, birch, and maple. Cost is relatively high.

Washbasins

When choosing a washbasin, first decide what type you want: freestanding pedestal, wall-hung, separate basin (set into a counter top), or a one-piece molded basin/counter-top unit. If you want to set a basin into a counter top, you should know that there are three types: self-rimming, flush mounted with a metal rim, and recessed. The distinctions are illustrated below. After deciding what type of basin you want, choose shape, size, color, and material. Generally, basins are oval or round, but rectangular, corner, and other shape variations are also available. Sizes range from 11 by 11 inches, designed for small spaces, to 38 by 22 inches, designed to accommodate washing hair or delicate clothing. Most basins come in white and a wide range of colors, although colors can cost 20 to 40 percent more. Be aware that spots show up prominently on the darker colors, requiring frequent cleaning. Most basins come with holes predrilled for fittings, but some, like the recessed type, may require you to install fittings through the counter top. Materials used to manufacture basins vary. See Washbasin Materials on the facing page.

Type	Material	Comments
Wall mounted	Vitreous china Enameled cast iron Enameled pressed steel	Wall-mounted basins can be flush with the wall or have a ledge back. Plumbing lines show beneath this type of basin but the cost is relatively low, and the style might be just what you want. (See page 1 for an example of how these plumbing lines are featured in a bathroom design.) Install drain and faucet fittings before fixing basin to the wall. Supporting legs are rarely required.
Set in Flush mount with metal rim	Enameled cast iron Enameled pressed steel	Cost ranges from low to moderate. Aluminum rims are purchased separately. Frequently used with plastic laminate counter tops.
Recessed	Vitreous china Hand-painted china Pottery Enameled cast iron Enameled pressed steel	This type of basin is installed from beneath the counter and is generally used with tile or marble counter tops. It can, however, be used with plastic laminate tops as well. See the photographs on page 68. With tile tops, the basin is set on top of a plywood base, then tile is set over and around the basin edges.
Self-rim	Vitreous china Hand-painted china Enameled cast iron Enameled pressed steel	This type comes with its own rim, is easy to install, and offers a broad range of styles and sizes. Many of the larger and odd-shaped basins are self-rimming.
Molded	Cultured marble Vitreous china (small sizes only)	This basin comes molded with the counter top, and is made to fit on top of the vanity as one piece. Cultured marble varies in quality, look, and price. Comes with predrilled holes for fittings.
Pedestal	Vitreous china	These basins are regaining their popularity. Unlike wall-mounted basins, their plumbing is concealed in the pedestal. A variety of styles is available. (See page 16 for one style of a modern pedestal basin.) Because there is no vanity, storage must be considered separately.

Washbasin Materials

Type	Comments
Vitreous china	Easy to clean; scratch and chip resistant; acid and stain resistant; vast array of colors; heavy.
Enameled cast iron	Easy to clean; scratch and chip resistant; many colors; very heavy; sturdier and more expensive than vitreous china.
Enameled pressed steel	Easy to clean; many colors and sizes; fairly durable; very light; low price.
Cultured marble	Many different brand names with varying degrees of quality; vast array of colors, patterns, and basin/counter-top configurations; easy to clean; heavy; warmer to the touch than vitreous china, cast iron, or steel.
Hand-painted china	Not as resistant to chipping as other choices; many different shapes and painted designs; can be expensive.
Pottery	More rugged than china but vulnerable to chipping; available in earth colors.

Washbasin Fittings

The two main types of washbasin fittings are spread-fit and center-fit (see below). Styles vary considerably, and price depends on both style and material. The most common materials are polished or brushed chrome, brass, and gold. The least expensive are the simple polished chrome fittings.

Type	Comments
Spread-fit (8 inches)	Spread-fit faucet fittings have one spout and two handles, each independent of the others. Slightly more expensive than center-fit type.
Center-fit (4 inches)	Center-fit faucet fittings have one spout and two handles mounted together on a single plate.
Single control (4 inches)	Offered on center-fit models, a center control operates hot and cold and on and off.
Drain assembly	Most faucet-fitting sets can be purchased with or without a pop-up drain assembly. If without, the drain-hole ring and rubber stopper are purchased separately.

SHOPPING GUIDE

Showers

There are a number of ways to create a shower unit in your bathroom: Combine it with a bathtub, using a built-in or attached showerhead; install a self-contained shower unit; install a shower pan (floor) and build the walls around it; or install your own custom shower pan and walls. The features of these alternatives are outlined below.

Type and Size				Materials	Colors	Comments
Self-contained units						
Square				Plastic reinforced with fiberglass. Comes with or without molded floor.	About 10 different colors	Self-contained units have their own walls but must also be supported with structural walls—the advantage is that no tiling is required. Drain pans are generally included. Some have ceilings. Some have doors, others don't. Some have molded seats, soap dishes, and ledges. All require non-abrasive cleaners. Fiberglass-reinforced plastic is more expensive than enameled tin or steel.
Corner				Enameled tin	White	Enameled tin units are inexpensive and easy to install, but can be noisy. They chip easily and are susceptible to rust.
				Enameled steel	White	Enameled steel units are moderately expensive, easy to install, less noisy than tin, but can still chip.
Shower pans						
Square	Rectangular	Corner		Molded stone. Terrazo. Acrylic (uncommon).	About 6 different colors	Offered in standard sizes. Can be used with prefabricated or do-it-yourself shower surround. Comes with drain hole pre-drilled. Offered with slip-resistant flooring that should not impede flow of water down the drain. From 5 to 6 inches high. Accommodates 2-inch drainpipe. Can be difficult to clean.
	Custom			Tile	Limited only by tile colors.	Custom showers can be of any size or shape. Tile floor needs a waterproof surface underneath, commonly made of sheet rubber, tar paper, or other waterproof material. Check local code requirements.
Tub/shower combination Built-in				Tile wall. Plastic laminate or fiberglass tub surround.	Limited only by material used for walls.	Adding a showerhead is inexpensive compared to installing a separate shower unit. The built-in showerhead looks like an integral part of the tub but is harder to install than shower attachments.
Attachment				Walls same as built-in.	Same as built-in.	A flexible showerhead is attached to the tub spout and can be hand-held or held by a bracket. Least expensive way to add a shower to your tub. Flexibility allows you to use spray head to clean tub or bathe pets. Disadvantages are that pipe shows, you have to hook it onto tub spout, and walls need to be waterproofed.

Shower Doors

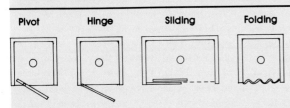

Pivot   Hinge   Sliding   Folding

If you purchase a self-contained shower unit, the door may come with it. Otherwise, you'll have to purchase the door separately. Frames are commonly made of chrome, but brass and brushed gold are also available. Material used for the door itself is usually plastic or tempered safety glass. They both come in a narrow range of colors and textures. Available styles are illustrated at left.

Bathtubs

Bathtubs are commonly available in a few basic shapes and in three primary materials: enameled cast iron, enameled steel, and fiberglass. Shape, material, and size all affect price, and if you want color instead of white, you can expect to pay 20 to 40 percent more.

Shape and Size	Comments
Standard	Standard tubs generally come without finished ends and only one finished side—they are designed to slide between two end walls and against a back wall. Some also come with one finished end and may be called corner tubs. Other variations include: oval interior shape; sloped backrest; handles in the sides; molded tub surround (see Wall Coverings on page 45). Sizes and materials vary.
Clawfoot	If you are creating a Victorian-style bathroom, the clawfoot tub is ideal. Some manufacturers make modern versions, and originals can still be found at salvage yards and sometimes at fixture refinishing companies. Be aware that the plumbing lines show and dirt will collect underneath. These tubs are always made of cast iron.
Corner	The longest dimension on a corner tub is only 4 feet, as opposed to 5 feet on a standard tub, but because the tub itself is set at an angle, you can bathe without feeling cramped. Corner tubs are made of enameled cast iron. Many manufacturers have discontinued this style, but it is still available in some places.
Molded platform	Molded tubs are made of fiberglass with either a gel-coat or an acrylic surface. The acrylic surface has deeper, richer colors. Shapes can vary from rectangular and circular to something as unique as a shamrock shape. These tubs are designed to be dropped into the floor or into an on-site waterproof box. Many are available with whirlpool jets.

Bathtub Materials

When you're thinking about a new tub, your first considerations may be shape, size, and color, but the tub's material can affect the durability, sound, feel, and color availability. Here are some salient features of each of the three main types of materials used in manufacturing tubs.

Type of Material	Durability	Colors	Cost	Comments
Enameled steel	Very long-lasting, but doesn't feel as solid as cast iron.	Primarily white. Other colors available through special order.	Least expensive of the materials.	Comes in variations on the standard shape only. Lighter and less expensive than cast iron, but more likely to dent on impact. Can be noisy unless treated for sound-deadening. (You can treat a steel tub yourself by applying 2 to 3 coats of auto-undercoating to the underside or by using insulation material.)
Fiberglass	With proper care, can last as long as steel or cast iron.	Wide variety. Deeper colors available in acrylic-coated fiberglass.	Medium to expensive depending on style and color.	Fiberglass tubs are lighter than metal tubs and won't chip, but they need a special cleaner to avoid scratching and wearing the finish. Some come with a tub surround. Available in a wide variety of shapes.
Enameled cast iron	Extremely durable.	Wide variety.	Most expensive of the materials.	These come in a variety of shapes and sizes. They retain heat well, are resistant to stains, chips, and scratches, and are easy to maintain. On the other hand, they can weigh up to 1,500 pounds when full of water, so they need to be well supported.

SHOPPING GUIDE

Tub and Shower Fittings

Spout and faucets can be mounted through the floor, a ledge, or the wall. You can separate controls for shower and tub or combine them, and separate hot and cold faucets or get a single control. Fittings generally come in chrome, brushed or polished brass, or gold. Waste and overflow assemblies are always purchased separately.

Type				Comments
Tub	Ledge mount			Mounted on edge of tub or tub enclosure. Usually 8- to 18-inch spread between handles.
	Wall mount	Single control		Operated by pushing, pulling, and twisting. Convenient because you need only one hand to operate controls.
		Two handles		Separate hot and cold handles. Standard is an 8-inch spread.
Tub/ shower combi- nation	Diverters	Diverter on spout		Can be pulled up and pushed down to divert water from tub to shower.
		Handle diverter		Twisting middle handle diverts water. Designed for 8-inch centers. Outer two handles control hot and cold water adjustments.
		Button diverter		Often found on single control faucets. Pushing a button diverts water. Operates on same principle as a ball-point retractable pen.
Shower	Single control			Operated by pushing, pulling, and twisting. Convenient because you need only one hand to operate controls.
	Two handles			Separate hot and cold handles. Standard is an 8-inch spread.
Waste and overflow assemblies	Pop-up			Operated by a trip lever, which causes a drain stopper to pop up.
	Grid drain			Operated by a trip lever. The blocking mechanism is not visible because it is inside the drain.
	Tip-toe drain			Operated by pushing down on a plug. When pushed again, it unplugs. Looks like a pop-up drain.

Toilets

Toilets are usually floor mounted. Wall mounted toilets require rerouted plumbing and 2 by 4 studs to support metal "chair carrier" braces. Toilets are made of vitreous china and bowl shapes are either round or elongated. Deeper colors are the most expensive.

Types of Toilets	Comments
Two-piece — Standard floor mount, Wall mount, Gravity flush, High, with bars	On any of the toilet styles, flushing mechanisms may be either reverse trap or siphon jet. Siphon jet is quieter. Some models offer a water-saver feature, which uses only 3 gallons of water per flush. It is quickly replacing the older, standard type, which uses 5 to 7 gallons per flush. The high toilet with grip bars is ideal for the elderly or infirm.
One-piece	Price of one-piece toilets varies according to style and color. Some have water-saver features. One-piece toilets always feature the siphon-jet flushing mechanism, and therefore are very quiet and have less chance of clogging than the reverse trap toilets. No wall-hung version is available. Most models offer the elongated bowl.

Wall Coverings

Since the bathroom is subject to high humidity, you should select wall coverings that are water resistant. This is especially true of the area surrounding the tub or shower. If water gets behind your wall covering it can rot the wall. You should also minimize this possibility by using waterproof wallboard behind the surface covering.

Type	Comments
Paint	Low cost, limitless range of colors, and easy application. Water-repellant paints recommended; however, enamel paint is not impervious to water, so is not enough on shower walls.
Wallpaper	Vinyl- or plastic-coated paper is recommended. Available in many different colors and patterns. Price varies according to design and quality. One roll 27 inches wide by 16 feet long will cover 30 square feet. Can be more expensive than paint.
Ceramic tile	Perfect for around the shower, but should be installed on a waterproof base. See page 46 for details on tile sizes and qualities. Can be very expensive, especially if professionally installed.
Tub surrounds Fiberglass	Tub surrounds are large sheets of material designed to be attached to your existing walls around the tub. Fiberglass surrounds can be purchased and installed separately or as a single package with certain tubs. Come in standard fixture colors and will last indefinitely provided you follow manufacturer's cleaning instructions. Inexpensive, especially if purchased with the tub.
Synthetic marble	At least one type of synthetic marble—Corian®—is available as a tub surround in a limited range of styles. Elegant look and durable, but is relatively expensive. Comes in a few shades of off-white and one variation has green veining.
Wood paneling and wood strips	Natural wood is susceptible to warping and must be treated to make it impervious to water. Treating both front and back sides works best. You can purchase wood in strips, usually made of redwood or cedar, which measure 3 inches wide and 4 feet long, sold in packages that cover about 16 square feet. Cost is moderate. 4- by 8-foot panels are also available, but do tend to warp.
Plastic laminate	Relatively inexpensive and easy to install. Many patterns, colors, and textures. Metal corners and seams.

Floor Coverings

Bathroom floor surfaces should be moisture and wear resistant, since they are subjected to a lot of water and heavy foot traffic. Vinyl is the least expensive, with carpeting next, and ceramic tiles running on the high side.

Type	Comments
Vinyl tiles	Come in 8- to 12-inch squares and sold by the square foot. Cheap tiles can wear out in two or three years; high-quality vinyl tiles can last up to five times that long. Easy to install and maintain, but if not installed properly, water can seep underneath causing them to buckle and your floor to rot. Many colors, textures, and patterns available. Some types have cushioned backs.
Sheet vinyl	Comes in 6-, 9-, and 12-foot widths. Can be more difficult to install than tiles, but the chance of water seepage is less. Depending on quality, can last for up to fifteen years or more. Usually comes with a cushioned backing. Some manufacturers recommend professional installation. Easy to clean.
Carpeting	Sold in rolls by the square yard. Nylon is the most popular choice because it is durable, resistant to moisture and stains, and can be washed. Available with or without rubber backing. Wool and other types of carpeting are not water resistant, tend to show stains, and wear more quickly under heavy foot traffic. Loosely laid carpet in the bathroom allows easy removal for cleaning.
Ceramic tile	Sold by the square foot and are available in many shapes and sizes (see page 46). Floor tiles can be glazed or unglazed, but unglazed tiles, unless very dense, should be sealed to protect them from water.

Tiles

Tile is available in a wide range of sizes, shapes, thicknesses, colors, and textures. Floor tiles are generally thicker than wall or counter tiles and more durable under foot traffic. The density of the tile material is often the determining factor in whether or not they should be sealed. Very dense tile (like porcelain) will not absorb water and thus makes sealant optional. Always buy a few more tiles than you need—if you need to make repairs, you'll have an exact match. Colored grouts can stain the tiles, but can also create a stylish effect. Some grouts are specially treated to resist bacteria and mildew. Tile installation can be easy or difficult, depending on the complexity of the area to be covered.

Type	Shapes	Sizes	Colors	Comments
Wall and counter Field tiles	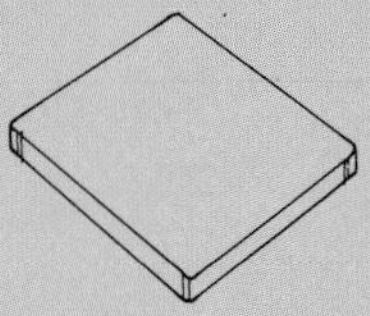	6" square 4¼" square ⅜ to ½" thick	Wide range.	Wide array of patterns, textures, and hand-painted designs from around the world. Usually glazed. Not recommended for floors because they're too brittle and thin.
Trim pieces	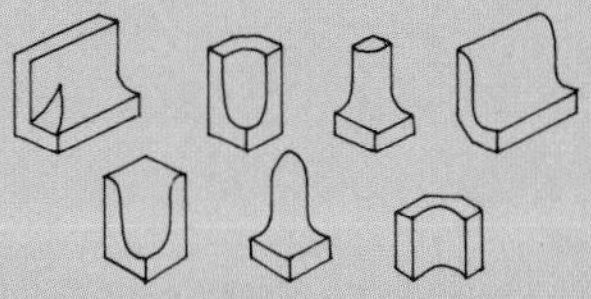	Designed for use with field tiles.	Made to match field tiles.	Same as above.
Floor Paver tiles	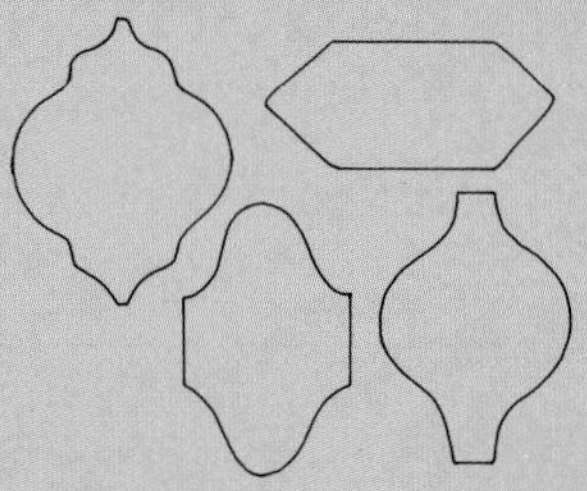	8"×8" 12"×12" 12"×6" 8"×4" ⅝ to 1½" thick	Earth tones. Limited colors.	Thickest of all tiles, most often used as patio or entry tiles. May be glazed or unglazed. Quite heavy and need adequate supporting structure.
Quarry tiles		6"×6" 8"×8" 4"×8" ½" thick	Earth tones.	All pavers are quarry tiles, but not all quarry tiles are pavers. Quarry tiles are never glazed and tend to be smaller and thinner than other pavers. Very dense tile does not require sealing because it does not absorb moisture. Can be expensive.
Marble	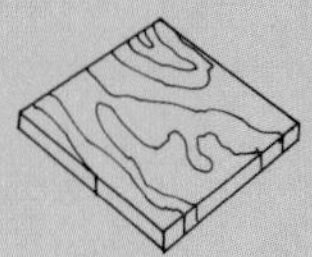	12"×12" ⅝" thick	About 15 different veining colors.	Very expensive, elegant, and as long-wearing as any tile. Color depends on where it was mined. Professional installation recommended.
Porcelain	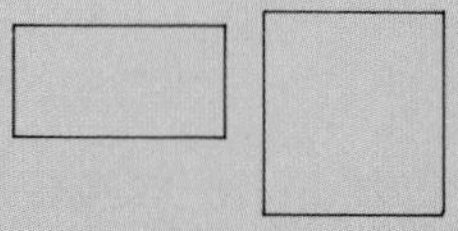	6"×6" 4¼"×4¼" 6"×8" 10"×10" 5"×9" ⅜" to ½" thick	Earth tones.	Very high density. Skidproof. Ideal for floors and counter tops.
Mosaic tiles	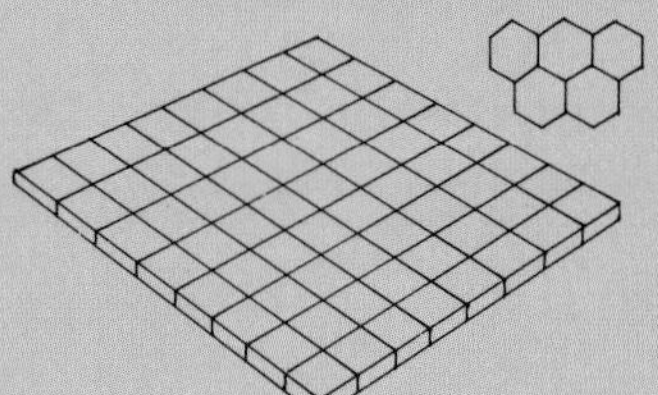	1"×1" 2"×2" ¼" thick	Many different colors, with or without glaze.	Stronger than wall tiles so they can be used for floors as well as walls and counters. Few trim pieces available.

Light Fixtures

When deciding on lighting for the bathroom, there are two types you should consider: ambient, or overall lighting, and task, or lighting that is directed to a specific area. Task areas are commonly the mirror, basin, toilet, and over the bath or shower. Wattage for ambient light should fall somewhere between 100 and 150 watts incandescent, or 60 to 80 watts fluorescent, and should be supplemented with task lighting. Light fixtures for the bath and shower should always be in a recessed vapor-proof housing, and all bathroom switches should be located far from water sources. The chart below describes some of the light fixtures that are available.

Type of Lighting	Type of Fixture		Comments
Incandescent Task	Single spotlight		Mounted on wall or ceiling. Fixture rotates, allowing you to direct light.
	Track		Cylindrical cans mounted to a ceiling strip. Cans can rotate and be directed toward specific work areas. More expensive than other types of task lighting.
	Make-up		Light bulbs arranged around the edge of a mirror. Pre-made strips are available for easy installation. Cost is moderate.
	Fascia		A long glass or plastic shield used for decorative effect and to diffuse light. Generally mounted on the wall next to or above a mirror. Lower in cost than other types of task lighting. More variety in length because size is not determined by tube.
Ambient	Ceiling fixture		Can be a hanging globe or glass or plastic fixture that screws into a plate mounted in the ceiling. Fixture should be moisture-proof. Low to moderate prices.
	Cannister		Shaped like a cannister and recessed into the ceiling with the bulb flush to ceiling surface. Moderate to high prices, and more complex installation, but very popular. Good for use above a tub or shower.
	Soffit		A box-shape shield attached to the ceiling, with a plastic plate placed under the bulbs to diffuse light. Some are plastic, others are made of wood. Price depends on material and size. Can range from 2- to 8-feet long. May be used for either task or ambient lighting and with either incandescent or fluorescent bulbs.
Fluorescent Task	Fascia		Glass or plastic shield used to direct and diffuse light. Mounted on wall. Lower in cost than many other types of fixtures. Comes in 18-, 24-, and 36-inch lengths for one or two tubes.
Ambient	Round or U-shaped		Fluorescent tubes bent in either circles or U-shapes.

When you think your sketches and product selections reflect what you want, you should do a cost estimate. These costs certainly include the beautiful new tub or basin, but they also include the ordinary—putty, wallboard, and whatever else you need to complete your project. If you already know that you want a general contractor to order your materials, now is a good time to hire one. Your initial materials list should include a variety of options. You can pare the list to your final selections after you speak with consultants, contractors, and suppliers. One of the best pieces of advice at this stage is: Ask for advice. The time it takes to learn about a potential purchase is far less than the time it takes to exchange it when it doesn't work or isn't what you really want.

What you pay for your materials depends on where you buy them. **Home improvement centers** generally cater to broad tastes, so their selections may be limited, but their prices are relatively low. Prices at **dealerships** are usually higher than in home centers, but the range of products is greater. If you look around enough, you will find exclusive designer fixtures, as well as fairly standard ones. The advantages of working with a **professional** designer or contractor are discussed below.

The Cost of Your Time

The one intangible element in these estimations is the cost of your time. If you find remodeling relaxing and pleasurable, you should certainly do as much work as possible yourself, but if you are pressed for time or find the work burdensome and unpleasant, you will be far happier hiring as much help as you can afford and then spend your time doing something else.

Before you can determine the time element involved, you need to have some sense of what the various jobs entail. Study the step-by-step procedures in Chapters Four and Five, which specify the work each task requires. You will have to estimate your own time for each task based on your skill and available time, but you can make some educated guesses. Then you can weigh your time against the cost of a professional.

Professional Services

If you expect to hire assistance, the following discussion may clarify what tasks professionals can handle at various stages in your project.

Architect. An architect is a specialist trained in structural planning. Unless you expect to move major walls or otherwise alter the structure of your building—in which case consult with an architect early—you probably don't need such a consultant.

Designer. Designers are concerned primarily with the present space. They oversee the general organization and appearance of your bathroom. Designers often work closely with a contractor to ensure quality work.

General Contractor. The general contractor will take responsibility for as much of the work as you care to pass on, including designing and planning your bathroom; stripping your old room bare; and buying and installing new fixtures, furnishings, and decorations. The general contractor's staff may do all the tasks, or the contractor

may hire any number of subcontractors to complete specific facets of the project.

Plumber. Unless you are highly accomplished at home remodeling and repairs, you will need this expert's guidance in rerouting pipes or adding new fixtures.

Electrician. If you must work with the major components of your electrical system, you are well advised to seek this professional's assistance.

Carpenter/Cabinetmaker. A carpenter is responsible for all woodworking, including repair and replacement of your subfloor, and a cabinetmaker can build cabinets to your specifications.

Floor Installers, Tile Setters, Glass Installers. These professionals are hired when you purchase your materials, and appear to perform only their special function. Often, the outlet that sells the materials will offer professional installation.

Licenses

In some states virtually all contractors are licensed; in others, almost none are. In some states only one of the company's principals or managers must hold a license for the entire company to be considered licensed. The business may then hire any number of licensed or unlicensed individuals to perform its work. Therefore, while a license may be important, other qualities, such as experience and the recommendations of satisfied clients, may be just as important as a license.

Why Hire Professionals?

It is immediately apparent that you might hire a professional to do a job that you do not want to do or that is beyond your abilities. But if you wish them to, virtually all professionals can supply the materials for their particular tasks. Moreover, professionals can buy materials at wholesale prices. Even if they mark up the materials, the price may be less than you would pay at a retail store. You will also find that certain manufacturers distribute their wares only to the professional trade. Often theirs are the higher-priced, unusually high-quality goods.

Professionals also assume full responsibility for the orders they place, subject to the terms of your contract (see page 53). They make sure each product is the correct size, shape, and color; that it is not damaged; and that it performs perfectly once it is properly installed.

Finally, a trained professional eye may detect problems or possibilities you have not perceived. Even if you expect to do most of the work yourself, you may want to use a professional consultant at various points along the way just to make sure you're on the right track.

Soliciting Bids

Although you may change your mind, you should make some rough estimates of what you want to do yourself and what you want to hire out before you solicit bids. Otherwise, you won't know what you're asking a professional to bid on. Just materials? Just consultation? Just labor? Or all three? You should also spell out how you want the estimate broken down. By categorizing the various jobs, including an estimate of the time each task will take, you will be able to weigh the professional's prices against the cost of your own time, and determine where you can save the most money by doing your own work.

When you know what estimates you want and how you want them submitted, you can develop a preliminary list of prospects by asking friends and neighbors for their recommendations, and calling contractors' associations or building trade schools in your area. You should always get at least three bids to ensure that you're getting the best deal. Although competitive estimates for small tasks may not be worth the bother, the difference between estimates on major jobs can amount to hundreds, even thousands, of dollars.

Getting References

When you've narrowed your list down to a few bidders, ask them for references. Call those people and ask if they were satisfied with the work your candidates did: Did the job get finished on time? Did the contractor leave the jobsite clean each night? Were all parties careful with the client's property? If possible, arrange to see the finished jobs and evaluate them for yourself. Money is not your only consideration when hiring a professional, and it is a waste of time to solicit a bid from one you might reject for other reasons.

Finally, call the Better Business Bureau, or some other consumer protection agency in your area, to make sure that a slew of serious complaints has not been lodged against the professional you're investigating. An occasional objection is nothing to be concerned about, but repeated instances of dissatisfaction are obvious signs of trouble. This is also a good time to make sure your candidate is licensed and bonded to perform the work you want done.

Getting the Estimate

When you've chosen your candidates, call them in to examine your bathroom and look at your sketches, materials list, and labor needs. Bear in mind that you may have to pay for estimates on large or complicated jobs. Be sure to ask about this.

Evaluating the Bids

When the bids come in, compare prices and schedules. Sometimes a conspicuously low bid omits something, and when it is added in, the bid may not be so low after all.

Reassessing Your Project

When you've evaluated all the estimates, you'll want to reassess the cost of your project. If costs are too high, you may need to scale down your project to something more affordable; if you decide you want to do more yourself, you may expand the timetable for the project. But ultimately you will achieve a balance of design, time, and budget and can make your final plans, draw up a list of the materials you will actually purchase, and develop your schedule. Then you can hire any professionals you need.

Checklist for Estimating Costs

The best way to estimate the cost of your project is to list all the individual tasks that it will include. Under each heading, list the materials, tools, and supplies you'll need. Then call or shop around to get prices. Such a list lets you know sooner rather than later which items cost more than you would ever have imagined—and which cost less. Further, as you think through each task, you may decide that you would like to try doing it yourself. This will also affect your estimate. Use the sample below as a guide.

Task	Items needed	Have	Buy	Rent	Price/ unit	No. units	Estimated total cost
Install tub	White tub		X				
	Fittings		X				
	Dolly			X			
	2 by 4 runners	X					
	Insulation		X				
	Joint tape		X				
	Plumber's putty		X				
	Caulking gun	X					
	Caulk		X				
Install tiles around tub, at base of wall, and in shower	Gray field tiles		X				
	Gray trim tiles		X				
	Tile nippers		X				
	Tile saw?			?			
	Layout rods	X					
	Compass dividers		X				
	Plumb line	X					
Etc.							

THE WORKING DRAWING

After you've reassessed your costs, incorporated any changes you want to make in your plans, and selected your materials, prepare a final drawing that includes the actual alterations and elements you have decided upon. Your working drawing should be entirely accurate but it does not have to be professional. Most building departments want to see a clear floor plan of the existing area and another of the proposed changes. Elevations and "sections" (details of interior structural elements) may be required in special cases but probably not for a project like the one illustrated here. It's a good idea to include the areas immediately surrounding the bathroom to show how the changes affect the use of the house. In most cases construction details are not necessary, but for alterations that may require substantial structural changes, a detail of the change should be included. Changes in interior wall structures and in window sizes can usually be covered with notations on the plan.

To obtain a plumbing permit, you should show the locations of the fixtures. Some building departments may want to see more, but you should start with the locations. The field inspector is the one who makes sure code requirements are met in the actual installation. The requirements for electrical permits vary, but you should show all light fixtures, switches, and outlets on your plan. Note any special circuits you need—a whirlpool bath might need a separate circuit, for example. GFI (Ground Fault Interrupter) receptacles are re-

quired near washbasins. For your own purposes, you may want to sketch out your final plans in elevation and call out the actual materials you've decided to use. These will help you make sure you order everything you need.

Your Materials List

Using your cost estimate list and elevation sketches as a starting point, you can make up a final materials list that will include all the information you need to order the specific items you have chosen. "White counter top" is no longer sufficient—is it plastic laminate, synthetic marble, or tile? For each item, you'll find it helpful to have the following information:

- Manufacturer
- Name and Model Number
- Color (be very specific)
- Material
- Size or Measurements
- Quantity
- Unit Price
- Total Price (plus tax and delivery charges)
- Date of Order
- Name of Individual through whom you ordered
- Projected Date of Delivery
- Second Choice

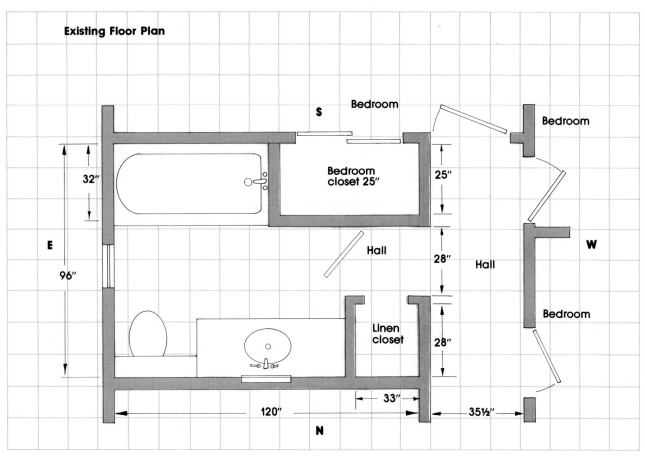

Existing Floor Plan

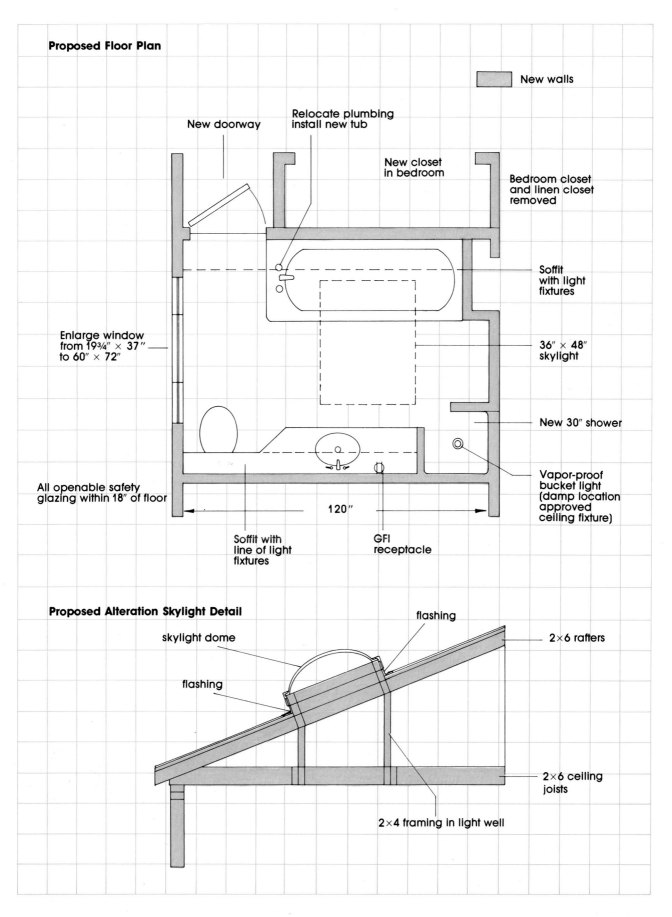

Proposed Floor Plan

New walls

New doorway

Relocate plumbing install new tub

New closet in bedroom

Bedroom closet and linen closet removed

Soffit with light fixtures

Enlarge window from 19¾″ × 37″ to 60″ × 72″

36″ × 48″ skylight

New 30″ shower

Vapor-proof bucket light (damp location approved ceiling fixture)

All openable safety glazing within 18″ of floor

120″

Soffit with line of light fixtures

GFI receptacle

Proposed Alteration Skylight Detail

flashing

skylight dome

2×6 rafters

flashing

2×6 ceiling joists

2×4 framing in light well

SCHEDULES & CONTRACTS

Schedules

It would be nice if you could order all your materials at once and have the ones you need arrive on your doorstep exactly when you are ready for them. Unfortunately, real life works a little differently. Contractors rarely start work on a remodeling job until they have everything in hand. They know that they will probably have to stop for extra screws or different hinges, but they go to great lengths to limit such extra stops. Unless you want to risk waiting a few months for that basin you thought would be delivered the second day, follow their lead: Make a place in your basement, backyard, or hallway to accommodate everything you expect to install. When it is waiting for you, instead of the other way around, begin your work.

Before you stash your new materials away for future use, open every carton and inspect each fixture or other piece of equipment to make sure it is what you ordered and is undamaged. When you've waited three months for your washbasin, it's unpleasant to discover that it's cracked but even worse to discover the fault just when you're ready to begin installation. When you've examined a piece and are satisfied with its condition, repack it in the original carton before putting it away.

Scheduling particular jobs depends on your skills as a handyperson and on the nature of the work you anticipate doing. If you are remodeling an older building, you are more likely to encounter surprise problems during your labors than if you are remodeling a newer one. Diverting the plumbing can be done quickly and without remarkable difficulties, or it can demand unexpected work on the system and the walls. If you have two left thumbs, even replacing a toilet seat can be a half-hour job, though under most circumstances it should take only about ten minutes. The amount of time a job requires may also depend on the number of helpers you can enlist. The additional pair of hands may make no difference at all in the length of time it takes you to install your toilet; but it can reduce your tiling time by a third or more; and without several other bodies, you could be all week installing a cast-iron bathtub.

The variables are so many that the best way to schedule your project is to break the job down into phases (see pages 55) and each phase into specific tasks. Make a flow chart to give you a quick overview of the entire project. Then, estimate the amount of time you think it will take you to do each task and double that estimate—most tasks usually take twice as long as you think they will. The flow chart/schedule will enable you to estimate the amount of time your household will be disrupted, to schedule your contracted services, and to make necessary adjustments in order to meet any deadlines you've set for yourself.

Contracts

When you've calculated your schedule, recontact the professionals you want to hire. If you're using a general contractor to oversee all the work, including the scheduling, obviously you will have already done so.

But if you want to use contractors only for specific tasks, now is the time to hire them. No matter how much you trust your contractor, you should always write a contract. Every term the two of you agree on should be in writing, and everything you want covered should be included. Anything you do not understand should be clarified to your satisfaction.

Contract Forms

Ordinarily, general contractors will have a standard contract form. These forms tend to be written in very broad terms, with a lot of open spaces to fill in. Contracts are intended to be discussed and negotiated: They are starting points—until they are signed. Then they are binding.

Sometimes the heading for a standard form agreement will read "Proposal," rather than "Contract." In content there may be no difference between the two documents, but in a court of law—should you find yourself in one—the heading can make the difference between a document that will be enforced ("Contract") and one that will not ("Proposal"). When hiring a professional, sign a contract, even if you have to amend the form's heading.

In the event that your contractor does not have a standard form or you dislike the form he has, you can take the initiative and create your own, to be certain you both know what you're signing, and to avoid unpleasant surprises.

Work Arrangement

There are many ways to work with a contractor but they generally fall into two main categories: Total Price, and Time and Materials.

Total price. A total-price arrangement means the contractor charges you a bottom-line figure that includes everything. It can be one amount for the entire project or individual amounts for separate phases of the project. The advantage of this approach is that you know how much the job is going to cost before you start. The disadvantage is that the total will include a hidden markup—as much as 25 percent—to cover unforeseen problems. This is not refunded even if the job goes smoothly.

Time and materials. A time and materials arrangement means that the contractor charges you an hourly rate for labor, the cost of materials, and a standard markup (usually 15 percent) for overhead and profit. The advantage of this approach is that you pay only for what you get. Your invoice clearly shows the amount of time worked, the cost of materials, and the markup. The disadvantage is that you don't know exactly how much the remodeling will cost until it is finished.

If you work on a time and materials basis, make sure you are clear about what the 15 percent markup includes and what it doesn't. For example, if you do the running around and pick up the materials but charge them to the contractor's account, will you still pay the markup fee? If you pay for C.O.D. materials ordered by the contractor, are they subject to the markup? Is consultation time charged separately or is it included in the overhead amount? Will workers supply all necessary tools or will you be charged a rental fee? Are plans included in the markup? Does the overhead figure cover the cost of replacing faulty materials discovered six months after the remodeling has been completed? Try to think of all the gray areas and make sure that they are understood and agreed upon by both of you.

Points to Cover in a Contract

It is hard to overestimate the importance of making sure your contract covers any problem that may arise. The following points should be included in your agreement.

Changes are the most common cause of misunderstanding and dissatisfaction. However carefully you have thought through your project, there are bound to be things you didn't think of and things you want to change when you actually see them. Be sure to agree in advance on how you will handle any changes in plans. This is especially important if you are working on a total-price basis: The smallest change can release the contractor from the original agreement. One method of dealing with such situations is to agree to make formal, mini-contracts for each change as it comes up. There will be few disputes if everything is down on paper.

Insurance. You should be prepared for accidents. Hopefully you won't have a fire that destroys all the lumber that was just delivered. But if you do, who is responsible for replacing it? Ask your contractor for certificates of insurance. If he does not carry any, you can buy your own for the duration of the project. Make sure the contractor carries workman's compensation—this is his responsibility.

Plans and permits. Determine who is responsible for supplying the building department with the correct documentation, for buying the necessary permits, and for arranging for inspections. Dealing with the building department can be laborious, and questions may be technical. It makes sense to let the contractor handle these details.

Completion dates. Even if the contractor will not commit to a specific completion date, make sure your contract ensures that work will proceed on a schedule. This might be a guarantee of a specific number of hours or days of work per week over a given period of time or until the project is completed.

Materials to be used should be written into the contract. They should include model numbers, sizes, colors, and manufacturers so there are no misunderstandings.

Payment. Decide when and how often you will pay your contractor. With a total-price arrangement it is common to divide the job into phases, paying an initial amount upon signing the contract, several intermediate amounts, and a final amount when all the work is completed to your satisfaction. If you are working on a time and materials basis, it is common to pay at the end of each work week.

This tiny washroom demonstrates how accessories can extensively alter a room that already has strong stylistic features. The gloss of the brass mirror frame and wall sconces, along with the curved water spout, provides a striking contrast to the rough-hewn adobe walls and counter and the handmade floor tiles. The choice of these accessories serves to give the room an elegant rather than an earthy feeling. The wall to the left, which conceals the toilet, might have been taken out to make a more spacious room. Instead, the owner chose to keep this small space to maintain an impression of intimacy as one enters the room.

DISMANTLING THE OLD BATHROOM

Before you can turn your new design
into reality, you need to take out the old.
Use the illustrated instructions in this chapter
to remove the old fixtures, fittings, and
surface materials—preparing your
bathroom for its great new look.

There are basically five construction phases of bathroom remodeling: demolition, rough-in, installation, trim-out, and finishing. Depending on the extent of your remodeling, you may emphasize one phase more than the others. But unless you are doing purely cosmetic work, which requires no installation or trim-out, you will engage in all five phases to some degree.

Demolition. During demolition your bathroom is stripped of fixtures, hardware, accessories, and any other items that will be replaced. If you are remodeling your entire bathroom, you will strip the room bare. In some places you may even open up the walls to repair or divert plumbing and wiring, or to repair the wall itself.

Rough-in. Rough-in includes preparing your demolished space for the installation of new fixtures. This is the time to replace sections of the wall that are suffering from dry rot, relocate any pipes or electrical wires, or install new lines, and build frames for partitions, closets, or medicine cabinets. If you want assistance with specific jobs, this is the best time to use professionals.

Installation. During installation you set all your bathroom's principal pieces in place except the toilet. Because the toilet is set on top of the finished floor, it is one of the last jobs you do. During the installation phase you should also replace old flexible supply lines and old or broken shutoff valves.

Trim-out. When all your fixtures are in place except the toilet, and all the basic wiring has been done, hook up the plumbing for your fixtures and connect your electrical outlets, switches, and lights. It is best to have all your fittings and related hardware in hand before beginning trim-out. What you saw in the store two months ago may not be there any longer. During trim-out you also install your medicine cabinet, glass shower door, and other units that are part of the bathroom's functional structure.

Finishing. The finishing phase is made up of miniphases. First, you complete work on your wall surfaces, including tiling, painting, and papering. Then you move on to the floor. It is important to have your subfloor properly nailed down. A smooth subfloor will eliminate squeaks, bumps, and wells in your finished floor. If it seems like too much of a bother to rip out your old floor, it is often possible to place a new subfloor over the old surface. The quality of your subfloor is particularly important if you plan to use vinyl tiles or some other flooring that allows water to seep underneath. As with the walls around your shower, you must take precautions to keep the framework free from water, and hence free from rot. When your floor is finished, you install the toilet, which is one of the easier jobs in bathroom remodeling. Finally, bring in your accessories, light some candles, bring in a good book, and relax for a long, hot soak.

Utility Lines

Before you start the demolition phase locate your plumbing shutoff valves and electrical service panel. In the event of an emergency, you will want to shut off all the power and/or water to your building.

Plumbing

The main plumbing valve is generally located outside, next to the building. Look for pipes to help you locate it. If you cannot find this valve, the city's shutoff valve for your house is usually located in front of your building, either in the sidewalk or in the grass nearby. It is covered by a metal or concrete plate that says WATER. Remove the plate by inserting a screwdriver and prying it

Remodeling does not necessarily mean removing everything old. Here, the antique shower fitting becomes a central feature in this otherwise modern bathroom. The clear shower curtain avoids obscuring the fitting's intricate lines. For additional photos, see pages 94-95.

up. Shut off the water by turning the valve counterclockwise with a wrench. To turn the water back on, turn the valve clockwise.

Capping pipes. In some older houses where the plumbing has not been modernized, it may be necessary to turn off the main water valve to change a fixture. If this is the case in your house, you need not leave the water turned off completely while you work. After you have turned off the main valve, disconnect the fixture as instructed later in this chapter. Then cap the supply pipes and turn the main water supply back on, so you have water in the rest of the house while you work. Three kinds of caps are in general use: threaded, unthreaded, and plastic. All three kinds should be available at your hardware store or home improvement center.

Threaded caps fit threaded pipes. Some short iron pipes and connectors are threaded on the inside rather than the outside; these pipes require threaded plugs that screw into them. Make sure you buy a cap of the right size—measured by the pipe's inside diameter—and of the same material as the pipe. If you have iron pipes, stay with iron; if you have copper, stay with copper. Unless you have a special connection, joining two dissimilar metals will cause corrosion.

Some copper pipes are unthreaded and caps must be soldered on. This task requires a 14 oz. propane torch and a solder flux. Both the fitting and the pipe must be thoroughly clean. If you have little experience soldering, this may be one of several plumbing tasks you will want to hire out.

Plastic is increasingly common for drainpipes, but it is rarely used for supply lines. If you have any plastic pipe, it will probably be unthreaded. Glue the cap on with a PVC joining adhesive specifically manufactured for this purpose and sold wherever you buy your plastic cap or pipe. Be sure you get the correct adhesive. "ABS" pipe and "PVC" pipe require different types of adhesives that cannot be interchanged. Your salesperson will direct you to the correct one.

In newer American homes capping the pipes will not be necessary because most modern plumbing fixtures have their own local shutoff valves (also known as angle stops); those with both hot and cold water faucets have two valves.

Angle stops are located under your washbasin on either side of the large drainpipe. When you turn the faucet-like handle to the right (clockwise), you close off the water supply to the washbasin. When you turn it to the left, you open the supply again. The toilet's single supply valve (cold water only) is located in a similar spot. Before working on any fixture, close all the valves.

Wiring

Your electrical service panel is usually located in your garage or basement; if you have neither, it is probably in the small utility closet that also houses your hot water tank, well-pump, and other major supply fixtures. If power lines in your community are still strung outside on poles, follow the lines to your building. The service panel will be nearby.

Gas

In the unlikely event that you should inadvertently strike a gas line—in a common wall between your bathroom and kitchen, for instance—you should be able to turn off the gas immediately. In most houses the main gas switch will be located right near the gas meter, usually in the basement, garage, or utility room.

Gas Meter

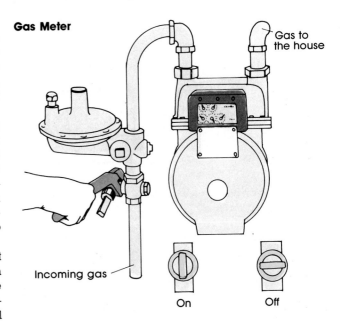

Gas to the house

Incoming gas

On   Off

Removing Fixtures

As you move through the first half of this chapter, you'll discover that removing bathroom fixtures is largely a matter of unscrewing the bolts that hold them in place. However, taking fixtures out can be a damp nuisance, so keep a bucket and some old towels handy. Otherwise, you should be able to handle removing your fixtures with a few screwdrivers and wrenches. A basin wrench, or plumber's wrench, will allow you to reach those hard-to-get-at places beneath the washbasin. Particularly if you're working in an older building where the pipes have been in place for many years, use two wrenches when unbolting pipes: one to hold the pipe steady and the other to release the connection.

You will also need help to remove some bathroom fixtures. A cast-iron tub, for example, can weigh 500 lbs. and is awkward to move around as well. Even a fiberglass tub can weigh more than 100 lbs., and its shape and size demand four or more hands to maneuver it, no matter how strong you are.

Start your demolition by taking out all the little accessories you have attached here and there; then remove any obstacles that will hinder you as you take out your fixtures, such as the bathroom door. If the vanity and washbasin will be in your way when you try to take out the tub, remove them first. Lay a complete trail of drop cloths from your bathroom to the outdoors and to any other parts of the house you may be going. Things will get quite dusty and dirty very soon.

TOILETS

If you're moderately hale, this is a one-person job. The hardest part is lifting and carrying the fixture after it has been removed. Even though you will empty the toilet and tank of water, a considerable amount will be left in the drain trap; therefore, place an old towel or two in your bathtub or shower to protect the surface and lift the disconnected toilet into the tub, dumping the trapped water there. You may want assistance with this.

Tools: wrench; screwdriver or putty knife; pliers.

Supplies: old towels; sponge; masking tape; rags; new closet flange (if necessary); bucket.

1. Remove toilet seat and lid by unscrewing the bolts. Turn off the water supply to the toilet, either at the building's main shutoff valve or at the fixture's shutoff valve. Flush the toilet until both the bowl and the tank are empty, and sponge up the remaining water from both parts of the fixture.

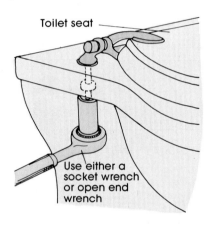

Toilet seat

Use either a socket wrench or open end wrench

2. Disconnect the water supply line by unscrewing the retaining nut at the bottom of the tank and the coupling nut at the local shutoff valve. Remove the connector pipe, and cover the opening to the supply line with masking tape until you are ready to install the new toilet. (This will keep the pipes free of dust and debris.) If the tank is connected to the bowl, remove the nuts on the tank bolts located under the rim at the back of the bowl. Some old toilets have an L-shape pipe connecting tank and bowl; if your toilet is one of these, unscrew the coupling nuts that connect the fixture to the pipe, and remove the bolts. If the bowl is also attached to the wall, remove the bolts that secure it there. Remove the tank from the bowl or wall, and set it aside.

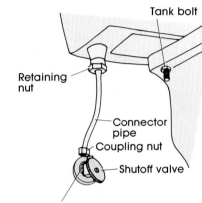

Tank bolt

Retaining nut

Connector pipe

Coupling nut

Shutoff valve

Supply line opening

3. The bowl itself is fastened to the floor by two or four bolts that pass up through the flange at the bottom of the fixture; these bolts are covered with small ceramic or plastic caps glued or puttied to the flange. Pry the caps off with a screwdriver or putty knife and remove the nuts.

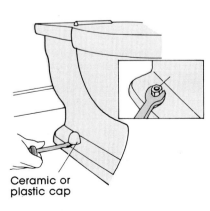

Ceramic or plastic cap

4. The bowl is now held to the floor by only gravity and a small watertight seal of wax or putty. Rock the bowl gently from side to side until the seal breaks and the bowl comes free. Lift the bowl off its bolts, gently place it on the towel in the bathtub, and tip out the water that remains in the trap. Set the bowl aside.

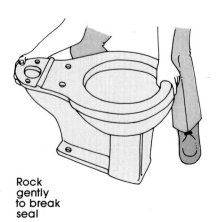

Rock gently to break seal

5. The metal flange, or "closet flange," around the drainpipe opening in the floor is now exposed. Slide the bolts out and scrape the flange and surrounding floor clean of the old wax or putty seal. Inspect the flange for cracks or other damage. If it has to be replaced, do so before you install your finish floor and new fixture. Flanges are available for about $5. Stuff the drainpipe opening with rags to keep it free of debris and to block sewage gas until you're ready to install your new toilet.

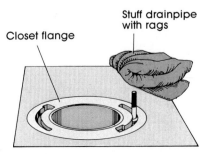

Stuff drainpipe with rags

Closet flange

BATHTUBS

The bathtub is the hardest of all bathroom fixtures to remove. Plan for at least two assistants. The size of your tub and bathroom may require you to remove the washbasin, toilet, or any other elements that obstruct its removal. If you have an attached glass shower door at the open side of your tub, you will have to remove that first (see page 63). If you have a freestanding tub, like the old Victorian clawfoot tubs, you can probably see all the plumbing connections. If your tub is set into one or more walls, it probably has a flange buried in each wall, and you will have to chip or cut into the wall all around the tub to remove the flanges from the studs.

Tools: magnetic stud finder or 6d nails; utility knife or saber saw; screwdriver; pliers; hammer; cold chisel; prybar; two 1 by 4 runners, 3- to 4-feet long; dolly.

1. If you have a freestanding tub, turn off the water at the shutoff valves and proceed to Step 3. Some bathrooms have an access panel to the tub's in-wall plumbing. It will be located near the floor on a wall adjacent to the plumbing end of your tub. The panel will be a simple piece of plywood, usually framed and painted over to make it inconspicuous. Pry the panel loose, and turn off the water at the shutoff valves. If your tub has no access panel, it may have no shutoff valves. There is no way to know without going into the wall. You can make a panel by cutting into the plumbing wall. If you find no shutoff valves, turn the water off at the main, and consider installing shutoff valves for future use.

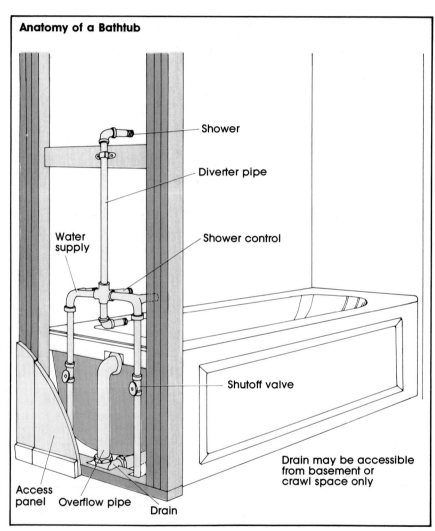

Anatomy of a Bathtub

Shower
Diverter pipe
Water supply
Shower control
Shutoff valve
Access panel
Overflow pipe
Drain
Drain may be accessible from basement or crawl space only

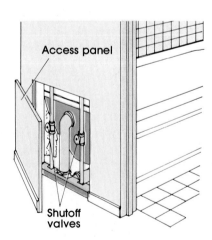

Access panel
Shutoff valves

2. To cut an access panel, locate the wall closest to the plumbing end of your tub. Find the two studs on either side of, and closest to, the drain. Turn off the electricity to your bathroom because you may encounter wires in the wall. Then, starting 2 inches above the floor or baseboard, use a utility knife to cut out the section of wall between the studs, which are spaced 16 inches on center in most newer houses and 24 inches o.c. in some older ones. Cut the section about 14 inches high. You can also use a saber saw for this task, but you are less likely to hit water pipes or cut electrical wires with a utility knife. Remove the section of wall, and close the shutoff valves. If there are no valves, shut off the building's main water supply. Plan to install shutoff valves for your new tub and to keep your access panel.

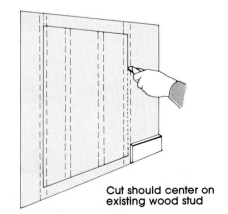

Cut should center on existing wood stud

3. Turn on the faucets, and let the water in the supply lines drain out. Remove the overflow plate, which is usually located just below the spout, and pull out the entire mechanism.

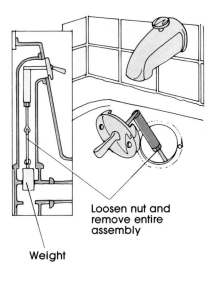

Loosen nut and remove entire assembly

Weight

4. Disconnect the tub from its drain-pipe by removing the drain strainer and the overflow control. You may have to pry up the drain strainer with a screwdriver. When the strainer and overflow control have been removed, insert the handles of a pair of pliers into the drain's crosspiece, and turn them counterclockwise. If necessary, use a screwdriver as a prybar to turn the pliers. When the crosspiece turns freely, you have disconnected the waste pipe from the overflow pipe. If the crosspiece resists all your efforts, you'll have to get at the pipes through your access panel.

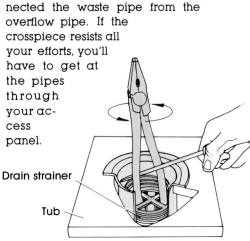

Drain strainer

Tub

5. Remove the faucet and spout assemblies from the wall. If yours is a freestanding tub, remove assemblies from the supply pipes and then remove the tub from the bathroom using two or three assistants and a dolly.

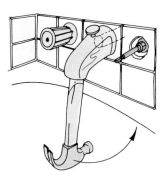

To remove spout, insert a hammer handle and turn counterclockwise.

6. To remove an in-wall tub, use a cold chisel and a hammer to chip or cut away the molding, tile, or other wall covering around your tub. Chip to a height of 4 inches or one course of tile, whichever is greater. (See page 66 for more information about removing tile.) If the flanges are anchored to the studs with nails or screws, remove them.

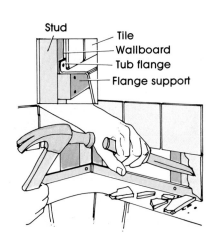

Stud
Tile
Wallboard
Tub flange
Flange support

7. Using a prybar and a couple of assistants, raise one end of the tub until you can slide a 3- to 4-foot length of 1 by 4 beneath it, all the way to the far wall; then do the same at the other end of the tub. Pry and pull the tub away from the wall until you or one of your assistants can stand behind it;

then pry, pull, push, and tilt the tub out of its recess. It may be necessary to stand the tub on end to get it through your doorway, in which case set it on the dolly outside the room.

Access panel

Shutoff valves

2 by 4 runners

SHOWER STALLS

If the plumbing in your stall shower is on a partition wall, you have to do some tricky work around the pipes. For specific information, see Ortho's *Basic Plumbing Techniques* or call in professional assistance. On the other hand, if the plumbing in your stall shower is located on a structural wall, at least two and perhaps three of the remaining shower walls are essentially partitions. If these walls are not encumbered with wiring, pipes, and duct work, you will be able to remove them without difficulty. However, most of the original walls in a house are likely to have some wires, pipes, or ducts, so you should turn off all systems and work carefully to minimize the possibility of damaging whatever components are lurking there. There is no certainty that a wall that is blank on the outside is also blank on the inside. The wall(s) you remove will throw up a good deal of dust, so you should wear goggles, work gloves, and a dust mask. Before you begin, turn off the water supply to your shower.

Tools: screwdriver; prybar; cold chisel; hammer; sledgehammer; circular saw; tinsnips or wire cutters; hammer.

Supplies: goggles; work gloves; dust mask.

1. Unscrew the fittings—faucets, showerhead, and controls—and set them aside. Then "skin" the wall by removing its surface materials.

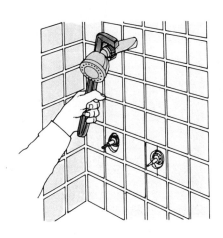

2. Use a prybar to remove plastic or fiberglass surrounds from the walls. You probably will not be able to salvage this material in any useful condition, but exercise special care not to damage the pipes when working on the plumbing wall.

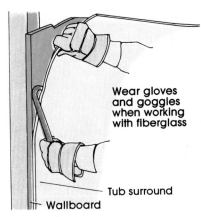

Wear gloves and goggles when working with fiberglass

Tub surround

Wallboard

3. Remove tiles from the wall with a cold chisel (see page 66).

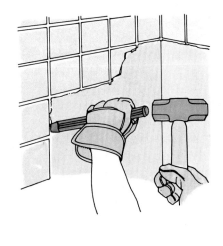

4. The inside of a shower partition is essentially the same as that of any small, nonbearing wall. It will be made of some combination of waterproof wallboard, plaster, studs, and lath. Break up the wall by pounding it with a sledgehammer. Work on only one side of the wall, and only between the studs. Whenever necessary, pull sections of the wall apart with your hands or prybar. If the wood lath resists, you can cut through it with a circular saw; if the lath is metal, use tinsnips or good wire cutters. Hammer along the studs to free any exposed wallboard, plywood, or lath supports, and push the wall through to its far side.

5. When nothing remains of the partition wall but its frame, saw through all the studs except those at either end of the frame, and push and pull each half-stud until it comes free from the top or bottom part of the frame.

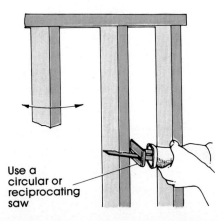

Use a circular or reciprocating saw

6. Cut through the end studs and use your prybar to pull them free from the walls to which they are attached. Work cautiously, and try not to fracture the wall surfaces of any adjoining rooms. Pry up the top and sole plates to complete removal.

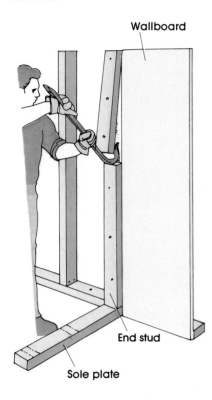

Wallboard

End stud

Sole plate

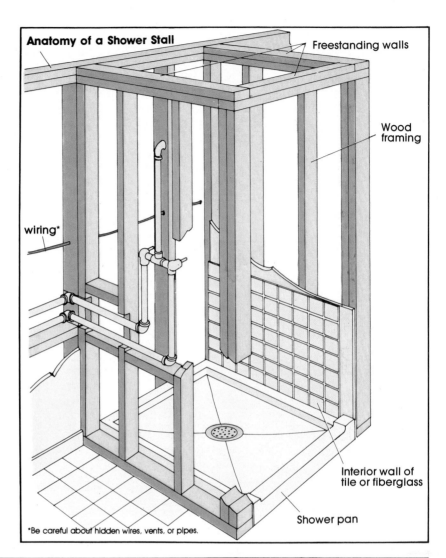

Anatomy of a Shower Stall

Freestanding walls

Wood framing

wiring*

Interior wall of tile or fiberglass

Shower pan

*Be careful about hidden wires, vents, or pipes.

Removing Shower Doors

If you have an attached shower door, you will have to remove this before you remove your shower stall or tub/shower combination unit. If you have a shower stall with a hinged door, you need only unscrew the hinges from the wall, remove the door, and unscrew the rest of the frame. Any parts that have been set with putty or other sealant will have to be knocked or pried loose. Sliding glass doors are not appreciably more difficult, though there is less chance of breaking the glass if you have an assistant hold them while you work.

Tools: screwdriver; hammer.

The doors slide on wheels set into tracks on the upper part of the frame. If possible, lift the doors off their tracks one at a time before doing anything else, and set the glass aside in a safe place. If it is not possible to lift the doors out of their frame, one person can raise the upper bar of the frame just far enough so a second person can lift the door from its track at the bottom of the frame. When the door is free from the lower track, lift the top wheels from their tracks. Carefully set the door aside. Repeat with the second door. You are left with a simple metal frame screwed or glued into the tub surround. You can lift the top bar completely free of the frame, then unscrew, knock, or pry loose the bottom and side bars.

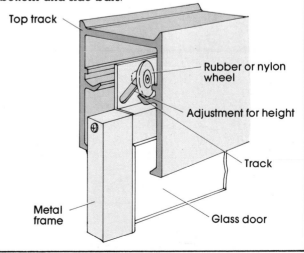

Top track

Rubber or nylon wheel

Adjustment for height

Track

Metal frame

Glass door

WASHBASINS & VANITIES

Bathroom washbasins, known as lavatories, may be wall mounted, set into counters, or free standing. Removal is identical for all types, except as noted below. The task is slightly more difficult than removing a toilet, but is still basically a job for one person with a little assistance. Turn off the water supply, either at the shutoff valves or at the main water valve. If you have a wall-mounted or counter-top basin, place a bucket underneath the trap, which is the curved pipe leading from the basin's drain into the wall. If you have a pedestal basin, keep the bucket handy.

Tools: wrench; plumber's, or basin, wrench; screwdriver; rubber mallet.

Supplies: bucket; length of rope; two sections of 2 by 4; masking tape.

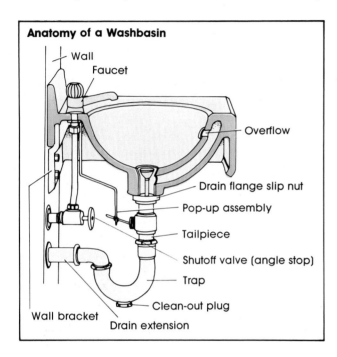

Anatomy of a Washbasin

Wall
Faucet
Overflow
Drain flange slip nut
Pop-up assembly
Tailpiece
Shutoff valve (angle stop)
Trap
Clean-out plug
Wall bracket
Drain extension

1. Turn the faucets on and drain the supply lines. Disconnect the water supply lines, first at the top (near the basin) and then at the bottom (near the shutoff valves), and seal the lines with tape until you are ready to install your new basin. If space under the basin is too cramped for you to reach the coupling nuts at the top of the supply line, use a basin, or plumber's, wrench.

Coupling nut
Supply line
Compression nut
Plumber's wrench
Shutoff valve

2. If the trap has a clean-out plug, unscrew the plug and allow the contents of the trap to drain into the bucket. Then unscrew the slip nuts that connect the drain trap with the tailpiece. If there is no clean-out plug, remove the trap, and tilt it into the bucket to drain it.

3. If your basin is installed below a counter top, set a section of 2 by 4 (several inches wider than the basin) across the top opening. Tie a wire or a piece of clothesline around the wood, and drop the line through the drain hole. Tie it around a second block of wood, leaving as short a line as you can between the two pieces of wood. Twist the bottom block until the wood is pressed firmly against the tailpiece under the basin. This will secure the basin until you are ready to move it. Then remove the lug bolts and clips that secure the basin to the counter. Finally, holding the basin from the bottom, slowly allow the line to unwind until the basin is loose. Then remove the basin through the counter-top hole.

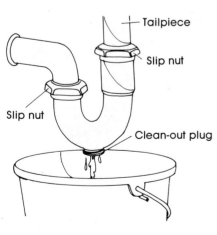

Tailpiece
Slip nut
Slip nut
Clean-out plug

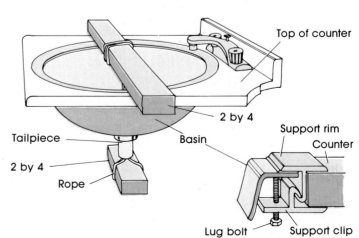

Top of counter
2 by 4
Tailpiece
2 by 4
Rope
Basin
Support rim
Counter
Lug bolt
Support clip

4. If you have a wall-mounted basin, disconnect all the plumbing lines, remove bolts, lift the basin straight up from its wall bracket, and set it aside.

Wall hanger

Wall-mounted washbasin

5. Remove the faucets by placing the basin upside down on a towel and unscrewing the retaining nuts from the faucet stems. Turn the basin right side up, and knock the faucets gently with a rubber mallet or the base of a screwdriver to break the putty seal that holds them to the basin. Lift the faucet assembly from the basin.

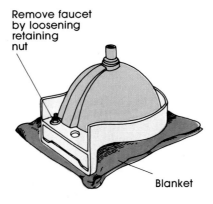

Remove faucet by loosening retaining nut

Blanket

6. If you want to retain your old basin but replace the faucet and handles, turn off your shutoff valves. Place a bucket beneath the supply lines and faucet connection. Then remove the supply lines. Using a basin wrench, unscrew the nut that secures the faucet. Plan to exert some force. The faucet assembly should pull right out. Faucet handles will simply unscrew from the top. Your new faucet and handles go in by reversing this whole procedure, including reconnecting the supply lines and opening the shutoff valves.

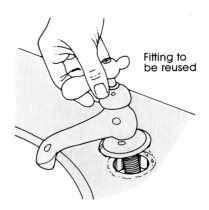

Fitting to be reused

Removing Cabinets

For the most part, removing cabinets is fairly straightforward work. The only unusual difficulties you are likely to encounter in this process will come from improperly hung cabinets. The cabinet, the wall, or both may be damaged when you remove the unit. Save the cabinet if you can, but repair the wall with spackle, plaster, or new pieces of wallboard. Be sure you have removed all fixtures and fittings before you begin.

Tools: screwdriver; prybar.

Supplies: spackling compound (for patching damaged wall).

1. Remove any drawers and doors so they won't swing open as you carry the unit away.

2. Remove the counter top (including the basin, if it is a one-piece molded unit). Whether your counter-top material is plastic laminate or tile, the surface material is applied to a plywood deck. You want to remove this entire deck, not just the finished surface. You can determine how the deck is attached to the vanity merely by looking up from underneath the counter top. Remove any screws. If the counter top is glued to the base, you may have to pry it off, and some older cabinets may need to be dismantled on the spot.

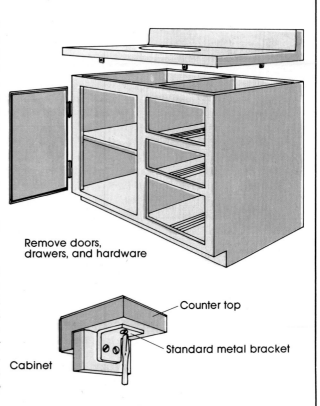

Remove doors, drawers, and hardware

Counter top

Standard metal bracket

Cabinet

OLD FLOOR SURFACES

Old floor coverings do not always have to be removed in order to install a new floor surface. If you want to lay new flooring on top of your present floor, the old surface must be absolutely clean of old wax, polish, dirt, and glue. It is also imperative that your old floor be smooth and even enough to accept a secure bond between itself and the new floor. Wood can be placed over vinyl, for instance, and vinyl can be placed over vinyl, if the old vinyl is smooth and even; but vinyl cannot be laid over ceramic tile because tile has as uneven surface.

Repairing surface flooring. If your old floor is sheet vinyl or vinyl tile, reset any loose sections, and use a premixed floor filler or spackling compound to fill in gaps caused by broken or missing areas. If the floor is curling or buckling, smooth it by regluing and nailing with 5d ring shank nails; or remove damaged sections altogether and fill in the missing pieces with floor or spackling compound. In all your repairs to your old surface, you are merely trying to achieve as smooth and even a surface as possible, so that your new surface will be received easily.

Laying a new subfloor over tile. If you want to avoid tearing out an old ceramic tile floor, you can simply lay a new subfloor of plywood over the existing surface. It will add about ⅜ inch to your present floor, so if the bathroom door swings into the room, you will probably have

to remove it, plane its bottom, and install a threshold. But you will still save time. However, you should add a subfloor in this fashion only if you know your present subfloor is sound and without rot.

Underlayment. Wherever your surface floor is seriously damaged, shows signs of leakage around a fixture, or seems to "give" when you press or step on it, you should remove a section of the finished surface (see page 65), and use a screwdriver to probe the underlayment (the material between surface flooring and subfloor—usually plywood or composition board). The screwdriver will sink readily into damaged or rotting underlayment, while strong underlayment will resist. If the underlayment is in need of repair, you must fix it before laying a new surface floor. Out of sight may be out of mind, but a rotting floor will continue to rot, whether you see it or not. The most common floor damage in the bathroom occurs around the toilet, but the instructions that follow are equally applicable to other parts of your floor.

Tools: screwdriver; circular saw; drill; saber saw; hammer; prybar.

Supplies: spackling compound; glue; 5d ring shank nails; common nails; ½- or ¾-inch plywood.

Laying New Floors Over Old

Wood over vinyl—ok

Vinyl over vinyl—ok

Vinyl over tile—no

Parts of a Floor

Surface material (vinyl or tile)

Subfloor (plywood or board lumber)

Underlayment (plywood or particleboard)

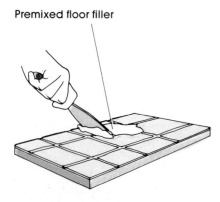

Premixed floor filler

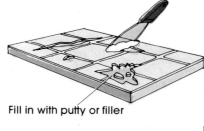

Fill in with putty or filler

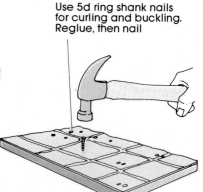

Use 5d ring shank nails for curling and buckling. Reglue, then nail

1. Remove a section of finish flooring large enough to uncover sound underlayment all around the damaged area. Take out the screws that hold the closet flange to the floor, but do not remove the flange or lean on it; undue pressure may weaken or break the joint between the flange and the drainpipe beneath it.

2. Using a circular saw set to the depth of the underlayment, cut out the section of underlayment you have uncovered. Remove the underlayment, being careful around the flange. It will probably be necessary for you to remove the underlayment in sections rather than all at once.

3. If the subfloor immediately below the underlayment is sound, cut a piece of plywood the same size and depth as the piece you removed. With a drill and a saber saw, cut a hole to fit around the flange, and nail the underlayment in place. You will probably have to install your new underlayment in sections rather than as a single piece.

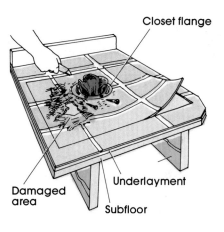

Closet flange

Damaged area

Underlayment

Subfloor

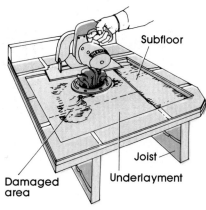

Subfloor

Damaged area

Joist

Underlayment

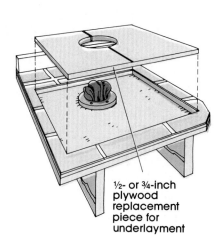

½- or ¾-inch plywood replacement piece for underlayment

4. If the subfloor immediately beneath the underlayment is also rotten, turn off all the electricity leading to the bathroom and connect your circular saw to an outlet elsewhere, using the correct heavy-duty extension cord. This is a precaution against sawing through live wires. If the subfloor is plywood, set your saw to the depth of both underlayment and subfloor, and cut out a section large enough to reach the nearest joists. Then replace the subfloor with

new plywood of equal thickness. Cut a hole in the patch to accommodate the flange, and nail the section to the joists. You'll probably want to cut the patch into two sections. Next, replace the damaged underlayment, but if you have to cut it, make sure its cut line will be perpendicular to the cut line in the subfloor patch.

5. If the subfloor is tongue-in-groove, cut each rotted board back to the nearest joist and pry up the boards. Remove any protruding tongues, and replace the boards with plywood and underlayment patches as in Step 4. Replace the flange screws to secure the flange to the floor.

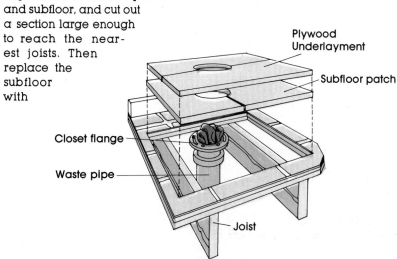

Plywood Underlayment

Subfloor patch

Closet flange

Waste pipe

Joist

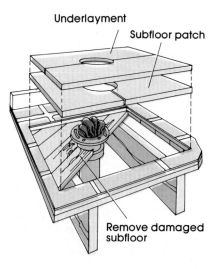

Underlayment

Subfloor patch

Remove damaged subfloor

REMOVING
TILE FLOORS

If your surface flooring is too damaged to repair in patches, if you have more than one layer of flooring material, or if you don't want to add an entirely new sub-floor, you should remove what is there now. It can be a messy job, but you need the results—a smooth surface.

Tools: Molding—prybar; screwdriver. Tile—mallet or hammer; cold chisel. Vinyl—household iron; putty knife; utility knife.

Supplies: old towel.

1. To remove all old surface floor-ing, begin by removing all baseboard moldings. Pry out wooden quarter-round with a small prybar or a screwdriver. This piece of molding is quite fragile and liable to snap, so if you expect to reuse it, be careful. Pry the molding out ¼ inch all along the wall; then go back to the beginning and pry it out some more. Repeat until the molding is free. Fol-low the same proce-dure with the some-what less delicate baseboard.

Plastic cove moldings will almost certainly have to be replaced in any case, so you can probably work with less delicacy and more speed—just pry them loose with a prybar and chip away at whatever small pieces remain behind.

2. If you are removing ceramic tile, start from an edge, using a mallet to tap gently on a cold chisel, removing one tile at a time. If there is no edge you can reach, you will have to make one, by breaking up a tile or two. Work gently, both to salvage as much of the old tile as possible and to minimize damage to the floor sur-face underneath.

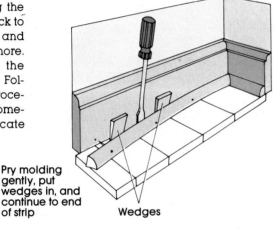

Pry molding gently, put wedges in, and continue to end of strip

Wedges

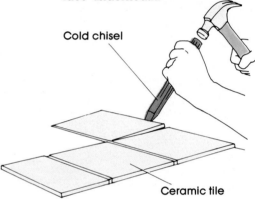

Cold chisel

Ceramic tile

3. If you are removing vinyl or similar sorts of tiles, you may be able to loosen the old adhesive by heating the tiles with an ordinary household iron. Use an old towel or similar cloth between the iron and the tile to protect both items. If you must pry up your old tiles, plan for a rather time-consuming and often tedious process. Use your prybar, mallet and chisel, putty knife, and any other stiff-bladed scraper you may require, and try not to dam-age the underlayment below.

4. If you are removing sheet vinyl or linoleum, follow the same pro-cedure described in Step 3. You will find it easier to remove this type of floor if you first slice the surface into strips or sections of a size you can handle simply. Use a utility knife with a fresh, sharp blade, keep your fingers out of its way, and then

remove the sections as you would remove tiles. When you have re-moved all your surface flooring, scrape up the little odds and ends of flooring material that want to stay behind, as well as any mastic or adhesive on the underlayment. This surface must be smooth and even.

Heat the tiles to melt the glue

Towel

Old vinyl cut into strips

Cleared area

WALL COVERINGS

You want to make your wall surfaces as smooth as possible. Remove old tiles and wallpaper, sand painted surfaces, and repair cracks and holes. If you're planning to install recessed items, a tub, or a shower stall, do so before repairing walls.

Tools: Tile—screwdriver; mallet or hammer; cold chisel.

Wallpaper—sprayer; stiff-bladed scraper; wallpaper steamer (optional). Paint—putty knife. Paneling—prybar; nail puller; hammer.

Supplies: liquid wallpaper remover; sponge; sandpaper; wire-mesh screen; spackling compound; epoxy.

1. Remove tile walls in exactly the same way as tile floors. You may have wall damage caused by moisture accumulating behind the tiles. Repair minor damage as shown below. Before removing tiles, take off accessories. Metal accessories, attached with screws, are easily removed, but you will have to chip ceramic accessories free. If you want to save them, be careful, but don't count on happy results.

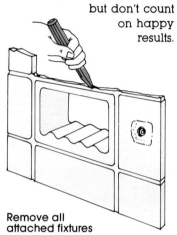

Remove all attached fixtures

2. Remove stubborn patches of wallpaper by spraying them with a liquid wallpaper remover solution—enough for the moisture to reach the paste underneath. Scrape the soaked paper from the wall, beginning at the floor and working at an angle toward the ceiling. If spraying doesn't loosen the paper, soak a sponge in the so-

Wallpaper remover solution

lution, apply directly to the paper, and then scrape; if all fails, rent a steamer. If your old wall surface is paint, you should chip away any loose, flaking areas with a putty knife, and sand the areas immediately surrounding them very lightly so that new paint will adhere to your wall.

Scrape softened paper from wall

3. Remove paneling with a prybar and nail puller. Sometimes the glue will pull off sections of the wall. Work carefully to minimize this problem.

Old paneling

4. Repair cracks or holes in the wall before applying a new wall surface. Small holes can be spackled over and allowed to dry. Open larger cracks farther, using a chisel or putty knife, so that you can clean them out and smooth their edges before patching. If the holes or cracks are too large to use spackling compound, buy a small section of ordinary window screen or some other wire mesh in a nonrusting material. Cut a piece slightly larger than the hole you want to patch, and push it into the hole. Bind it to the inside of the wall with in-

stant-bond glue or epoxy. When it has set, patch over the mesh with spackling compound or plaster. In the event that the wall beneath your paper is seriously damaged, you may need to perform more extensive wall repairs. For specific instructions on this kind of task, see *Basic Home Repairs.*

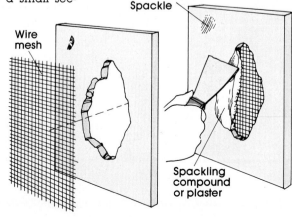

Wire mesh

Spackle

Spackling compound or plaster

INSTALLING YOUR NEW BATHROOM

You're in the homestretch.
Follow the step-by-step illustrations
in this chapter to bring your design to life.
When you've added the finishing touches, you'll
look around your new bathroom and wonder
how you ever managed without it.

If you're doing a full-scale remodeling job, your bathroom probably looks pretty bare right now. In fact, it may be stripped down to naked walls and plumbing stub-outs. But since you planned your remodeling activities according to a timetable as well as a design scheme and budget, the new items should have arrived on your doorstep, and you should be ready to put the components together.

The first installation step includes all the rough plumbing and wiring. As mentioned in Chapter One, you will find step-by-step instructions for these tasks in Ortho's books, *Basic Wiring Techniques* and *Basic Plumbing Techniques*. Because the bathtub sits directly on your subfloor and usually has to be screwed to the wall studs, it goes in during this stage. If you're building a shower stall, it, too, should be installed at this point. You'll also want to allow for any recessed shelves, cabinets, or accessories (see page 70).

When these elements are in place, close up your walls with wallboard. From here on, the order of installation can vary. One option is to finish walls and floor first and then put in the vanity. Another is to put in the vanity first and then cover the walls and floor. Which procedure you choose depends on the materials you're using and how you want to join one element to another. For

example, do you want a one-piece floor that extends under the vanity, or do you want to cut around the vanity and install a baseboard or molding strip? Because the order of these steps can vary, you may need to flip back and forth between the sections in this chapter to follow your own plan. Whatever sequence you follow, the toilet is always the last fixture you install because it sits on the finished floor.

For the most part, the process of installing plumbing fixtures is simply the reverse of removing them. As before, you will need assistance with the bathtub, whereas the toilet and washbasin really require but a single pair of hands. You will purchase almost all plumbing assemblies separately from the fixtures, so make sure that they fit and that you have the manufacturer's installation instructions for both the fixtures and the fittings. Follow the manufacturers' instructions, even if they differ from those in this book or in other manuals you may have read. The manufacturers know their own products best.

When tightening nuts, do most of the work by hand, then gradually complete the job with a wrench. If you go too far too fast, you can strip pipe threads and damage other materials. Anyplace you are making a watertight seal, use plumber's putty; anyplace you are connecting nuts and bolts, either wrap them in joint tape or cover them with joint compound, also known as "pipe dope." These precautions will help prevent annoying leaks. Anyplace you are wedding two pieces of metal in your plumbing system, make sure they are the same kind of metal. Iron and copper, for example, get along poorly together: They corrode one another.

Always turn your water off before working on plumbing fixtures, or you'll find deep puddles on your floor. When you've finished a plumbing task, turn the water back on and test your work. It is never fun to find a leak, but it is far better to find it while your tools are out than to have it spring upon you the night of your big dinner party.

A close-up of the vanity in the bathroom shown on pages 14–15 demonstrates the importance of details in installation. Here the counter tiles are installed flush with the washbasins to provide a clean line. Five coats of sealant not only waterproof the wood floor but also give it a high gloss consistent with the bold aspects of this design. Yet the wood shows through, linking the room to the deck and yard outside.

RECESSED CABINETS

There are two basic kinds of medicine cabinets: those that hang on the wall, called "surface-mounted" cabinets, and those that are recessed into the wall. The hanging kind comes with installation instructions; but even if it does not, installation is generally a matter of measuring where nails or screws should go, drilling a couple of pilot holes, and hanging the unit up. Recessed medicine cabinets are a bit trickier. When you cut the wallboard or plaster and lath, you may encounter wiring, water pipes, vents, structural framing for windows or pocket doors, or heat and air ducts. However, if you do not run into any of these obstacles, installing a recessed medicine cabinet is fairly simple. Studs are placed at 16- or 24-inch intervals, center to center. Thus, the actual space between the studs is 14½ inches or 22½ inches. And these are exactly the widths of many medicine cabinets. Ideally, you'll be able to work between studs rather than having to cut through any. Larger cabinets that do not fit between the studs will require extra bracing.

Tools: drill; utility knife; circular, reciprocating, or handsaw; hammer; level; plumb line; screwdriver.

Supplies: common nails; screws; 2 by 4s to size.

1. To install a standard-size medicine cabinet, determine where you want to place it, and locate the nearest studs. Measure the unit, and mark the measurements on the wall. Turn off your electricity to avoid cutting hidden live wires, and cut out the section. Toenail two sections of 2 by 4 to fit horizontally between the studs and flush with the opening you've cut. These headers, along with the studs, form your frame. Plumb and screw the cabinet within its frame, hang the door, and install hardware.

2. To install a larger unit, start by determining where you want to place the cabinet, and locate the studs closest to its outside edges. Measure the unit. Add 1½ inches top and bottom to accommodate 2 by 4 headers. If you are installing your cabinet in a bearing wall, add 3½ inches on top, plus the 1½ inches at the bottom. The extra space at the top is to accommodate a double header (see Step 3). Mark these dimensions on the wall, turn off your electricity, and use a keyhole saw to cut the sections out between the studs. It's easier to install the supporting frame when you cut the hole larger than the unit itself. But it also means you'll have to patch the wall when you're done. You may have an easier patching job if you remove all the wallboard above the cabinet in a 4-foot-wide strip. Be sure you make your cuts on studs so you'll have something to which you can nail the patch.

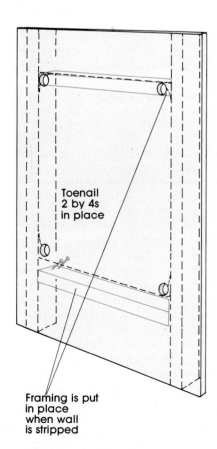

Toenail 2 by 4s in place

Framing is put in place when wall is stripped

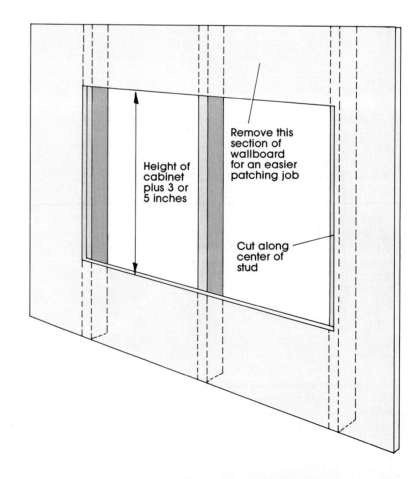

Height of cabinet plus 3 or 5 inches

Remove this section of wallboard for an easier patching job

Cut along center of stud

3. Cut any obstructing studs. Then cut and install the top header. To provide maximum support for the cut stud in a bearing wall, use a double header. Two flat 2 by 4s are sufficient if there is no more than one cut stud. Otherwise, sandwich a piece of ½-inch plywood between two 2 by 4s and install the unit on edge. Toenail in place and check with a level.

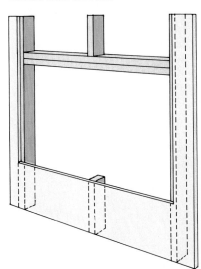

4. Next, install cripples. Measure the distance from the header to the floor, cut two 2 by 4s to length, and nail them to the two outside studs.

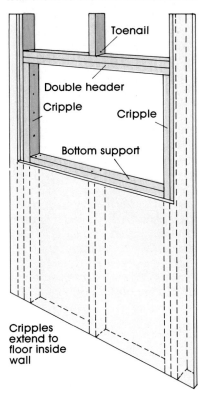

Toenail

Double header

Cripple

Cripple

Bottom support

Cripples extend to floor inside wall

5. Install the bottom support between the cripples. If you're installing a mid-size cabinet, add a filler piece and blocking to create the correctly sized opening for your cabinet. If you're centering the cabinet in the space, follow this procedure for both sides. Install the cabinet according to the manufacturer's instructions, plumb and screw the cabinet within its frame, hang the doors, and install hardware. Then patch the wall.

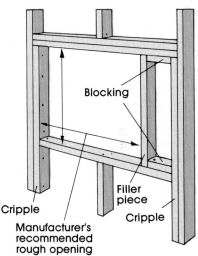

Blocking

Filler piece

Cripple

Cripple

Manufacturer's recommended rough opening

Installing Recessed Accessories

Medicine cabinets are not the only accessories that may be recessed in the bathroom. It is fairly common to recess toilet tissue holders, soap dishes, and even cup holders. Typically, an accessory designed to be recessed is made in two pieces: a brace and a face. Installation for all such items is basically the same.

Tools: utility knife and/or keyhole saw; level; plumb line; screwdriver.

Supplies: screws.

1. After you cover the studs with wallboard, use a utility knife to cut a hole ½ to 1 inch smaller than the overall dimensions of the outside of the face plate. Be sure you are cutting between the studs, not into them. Insert the brace section into the hole. Hold it in place with your hand as you bring the face plate up to it. Screw the front piece into the brace with the hardware provided by the manufacturer. The screw is designed to draw the brace and the face together, securing your installation.

2. If you want to install ceramic accessories in your tiled wall, simply open a space in the wallboard or mortar bed and set the accessory as if it were an ordinary tile. If you want to install a metal dish in a tile wall, complete your tiling first, but leave a gap slightly smaller than the accessory, and follow the procedure outlined in Step 1.

3. If your wall is already opened up for extensive patching or some other reason, you can toenail a 2 by 4 between two studs, and use it as a brace for screws. Few accessories require such bracing, but it is useful for items like horizontal grab bars near the bathtub.

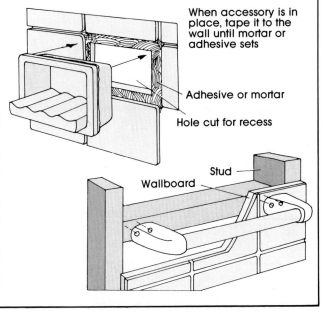

When accessory is in place, tape it to the wall until mortar or adhesive sets

Adhesive or mortar

Hole cut for recess

Stud

Wallboard

INSTALLING
SHOWER STALLS

In a small bathroom a shower may prove so much more practical than a tub that you may decide to dispense with the larger fixture altogether. You can use your old bathtub supply and drain pipes, and you may even keep the old diverter faucet rather than installing new plumbing. If you want to change the location of the shower, however, you will have to divert your supply and waste pipes to the area where your shower will stand. Unless you are especially adept at plumbing and are prepared to deal with unexpected difficulties, plan to get assistance from a professional or from Ortho's *Basic Plumbing Techniques* .

Prefabricated shower stalls. If you don't want to build a complete shower stall from scratch, you can purchase a prefabricated stall of plastic, metal, or fiberglass. Prefabricated units cost only a few hundred dollars, depending on material, size, and style; they include everything you need for a shower except the plumbing and water; and they can ordinarily be installed by one person in an afternoon. Before buying such a prefabricated stall, however, check its measurements, and make certain it will fit through your door.

Building a shower stall. For the most part, building an enclosure for a shower stall is identical to building any

other nonbearing partition or wall: Create a frame, secure the frame to the fixed walls around its perimeter, and cover the frame with an appropriate skin. The only difference between this and other partitions is that plumbing lines may have to be adapted or brought into the space before the walls are finished.

Before installing new plumbing, plan for any special features you might like. For instance, shower faucet handles are normally placed 42 to 48 inches from the floor, and showerheads are usually between 66 and 78 inches high. But if you are tall, 54 inches might be a more useful height for the handles, and you might be more comfortable with a higher showerhead as well. Other features, like multiple showerheads that are placed at different heights and activated individually or all at once, are also available. When you're building your own shower stall, you are limited by your imagination and budget only. Once your plumbing is established, creating a shower stall is a simple matter.

Tools: wrench; pliers; level; circular saw; hammer.

Supplies: drainpipe and hardware; 2 by 4s to size; nails; wallboard; interior and exterior finish materials.

Self-contained shower

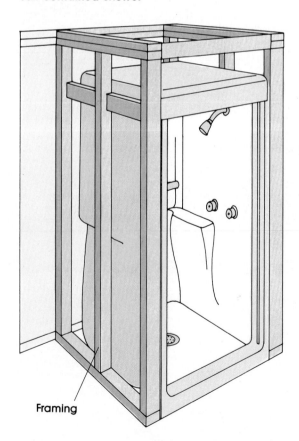

Framing

Custom built shower

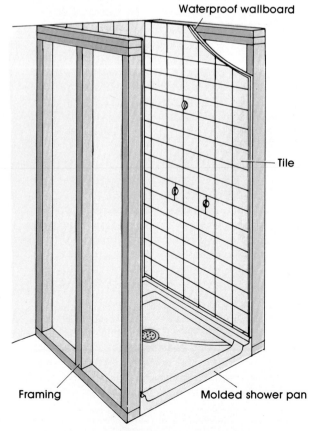

Waterproof wallboard

Tile

Framing

Molded shower pan

1. Standard shower bases are available in 32-, 36-, and 42-inch squares; other sizes can be custommade. Most such shower bases, or "pans," slope gently toward a central drain hole 2 inches in diameter, which can be fitted directly beneath the shower to an extension of the drainpipe. When your pan is positioned and leveled in both directions, and the drain is installed according to the instructions accompanying the shower pan, test your plumbing for leaks. This will be your last chance to correct mistakes easily. If the plumbing system is fine, construct frames for each necessary wall.

2. Make frames of 2 by 4s. Assembly is easiest if you lay them out on the floor. Place studs 16 inches apart and add 2 by 4 crosspieces (blocking) between them. When the frames are complete, raise them and secure them to each other, to the floor, ceiling, adjacent walls, and to the shower base.

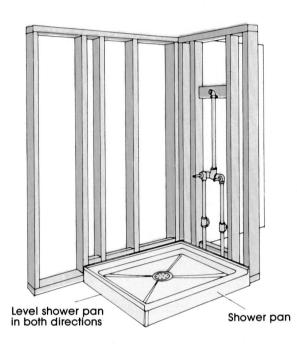

Level shower pan in both directions

Shower pan

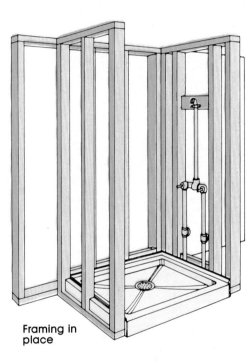

Framing in place

3. When the frames are in place, install ½-inch waterproof wallboard.

4. Finish the walls both inside and out. The outside finish will be part of your general esthetic scheme and is likely to be paint, wallpaper, or tile. See page 84 for information about installing wall tiles. The inside of your shower should, of course, be tile or some other surface impervious to water. Install a glass shower door according to the manufacturer's instructions, or install a shower curtain rod.

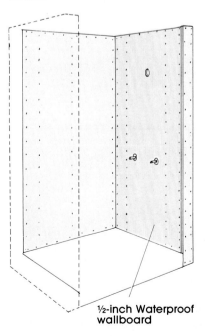

½-inch Waterproof wallboard

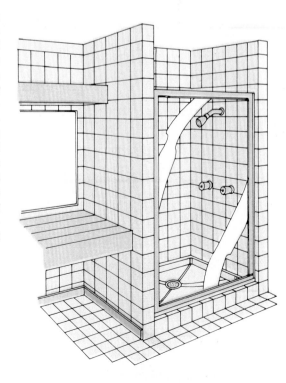

BATHTUBS

The tub is the hardest of all bathroom fixtures to install, for the same reasons it is the hardest to remove: It is big, clumsy, and heavy, and you almost always have to make some plumbing attachments in the wall. Because of the weight and bulk of even a fiberglass tub, you will need at least one assistant. If your tub is cast iron, you will need at least two helpers. The tub itself rests on the room's subfloor, so it goes in place before you lay your surface floor. You generally attach the supply and drain pipes after the tub is in position. The faucet, spout, and shower fittings go in when the walls are finished.

There are all sorts of bathtubs, made of different materials and varying in size and configuration. Each has its own peculiarities of installation, and you should be sure to get printed installation instructions from your dealer or the unit's manufacturer. The instructions that follow apply to the most common enameled steel fixture 30 by 60 inches. But even if yours is a different sort of bathtub, these instructions should provide you with a general sense of the procedures you will have to follow.

Tools: dolly; wrench; screwdriver; hammer; drill; caulking gun.

Supplies: 2 by 4 supports for built-in tub; common nails; shims (if necessary); roll of fiberglass insulation; two to three 1 by 4 runners, 3- to 4-feet long; fittings and hardware; caulk; plumber's putty; joint tape or joint compound.

1. If your tub does not come with a blanket of padding or insulation attached to its base, buy a single roll of fiberglass insulation at your home improvement center, and cut a section to fit against the sides of the fixture. The insulation cuts down bathtub noise and also helps the fixture hold heat longer. If there's enough space, you can put insulation under the tub as well.

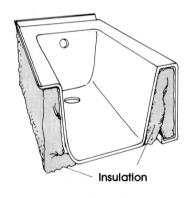

Insulation

2. Built-in tubs require 2 by 4 supports along the walls for the tub's flanges to rest on. Sometimes you can use the supports already in place from a previous tub, but you must measure heights very carefully. If there is any discrepancy, replace the supports. Otherwise your tub will never rest at a proper level. When the 2 by 4 wall supports are in place,

lay a few 1 by 4 runners where the tub is to go, and push the tub along these runners until it is in place. Then ease the runners out one at a time.

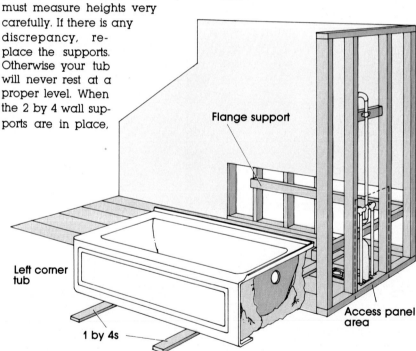

Flange support

Left corner tub

1 by 4s

Access panel area

3. Steel tubs can simply rest on the 2 by 4 supports, but the flanges of fiberglass tubs should be nailed to the supports. If the tub's manufacturer has not predrilled holes in the flanges, drill your own pilot holes before nailing to prevent the fiberglass from splitting. If necessary, shim the flanges so that your tub is not only level, but also stable. It should not rock. If for some reason you find it

impossible to level the tub perfectly, at least arrange for it to tilt toward its drain end, or you'll always have to bail it out after use.

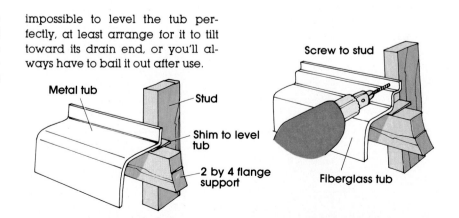

Metal tub

Stud

Shim to level tub

2 by 4 flange support

Screw to stud

Fiberglass tub

4. Attach supply and drain pipes, working through the access panel. Inside the wall you will install a mixing valve, following the manufacturer's instructions. The mixing valve allows you to control the temperature of your bath or shower water. After you hook up the hot and cold supply lines to the stub-outs, they will meet at this valve. The drain and vent line is a single pipe, 2 to 3 inches wide, that usually travels straight up and down inside the wall. Where it meets the waste overflow drain, it angles off and up through the roof to vent gases. Below the waste overflow drain, it runs into the tub floor drain, carrying wastewater to the sewer.

5. Install waste, overflow, and lift linkage according to the manufacturer's instructions. There are three kinds of waste/overflow fittings: (a) the rubber stopper you simply push into the drain; (b) the pop-up drain; and (c) the trip lever.

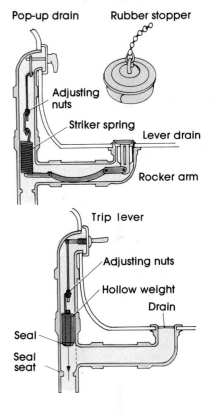

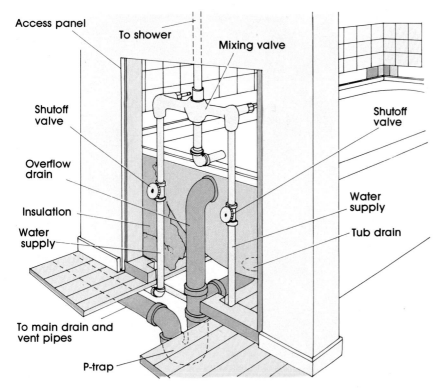

6. The faucet assembly for your shower should include a diverter and a length of pipe intended to run up inside the wall. It will end at the top in an elbow joint where you will attach another, shorter length of pipe and the showerhead. The shower pipe should be installed so that it ends between 66 and 78 inches from the bathroom floor, depending on your height. Remember that the angled pipe and showerhead will effectively lower the shower 6 to 8 inches.

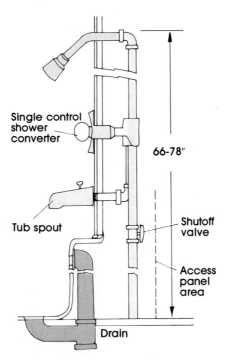

7. When the pipes are connected, install waterproof wallboard over the tub's flanges. Attach the faucet assembly according to the manufacturer's instructions. Turn the water back on and check for leaks. If water appears anyplace, tighten the fittings until the leak stops. Then caulk around the rim and base of the tub.

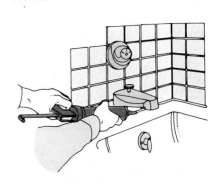

SIMULATED SUNKEN TUB

Sunken tubs conjure up images of resplendent luxury, but it is rarely practical and almost never easy to sink a tub in the course of remodeling a bathroom yourself. Filled with water, a tub can easily weigh a ton, and it must be supported. Ordinarily, the floor joists provide the primary support for a tub. To sink a tub, you must sever several of these stout timbers, build a new frame for the tub, and construct some additional support for the floor.

However, with a little ingenuity you can create the feeling of a sunken tub by raising the level of the surrounding area rather than lowering the fixture itself.

Tools: hammer; screwdriver; circular saw.

Supplies: 2 by 4s to size; common nails; finishing nails; toggle or molly bolts (if necessary); ½-inch CDX plywood or waterproof wallboard; white construction glue.

1. A basic tub enclosure is simply a frame made of 2 by 4s with supporting studs placed every 16 inches. Build one frame for each of your tub's exposed sides. The frames should be just enough lower than the rim of the tub to accommodate the combined thicknesses of a plywood covering and your chosen finish material. For example, if you want to finish the frame with tiles, which are generally ¼-inch thick, you would build your frame the height of your tub less ¾ inch—½ inch for a plywood covering and ¼ inch for the tile. When you cut the studs, remember to subtract an additional 3 inches to accommodate the top and sole plates. When your frames are constructed, attach them to the walls and floor with nails and white construction glue. Use toggle or molly bolts at the wall if your frame does not abut a stud.

2. To extend the storage ledge on any exposed side of your tub, merely build an extra frame identical to the first one, and set it parallel to the first frame as far away as you want your ledge to be wide. If you want a ledge wider than 16 inches, build another frame, and space the frames evenly so your ledge has adequate support at all points.

3. Cover the tops and sides of your frames with ½-inch CDX plywood or waterproof wallboard. Caulk all junctures of tub and frame. Complete with your chosen finish material.

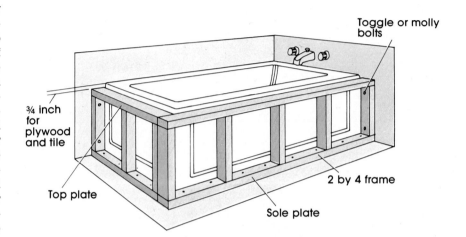

Toggle or molly bolts

¾ inch for plywood and tile

Top plate

2 by 4 frame

Sole plate

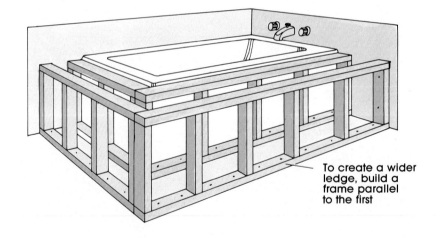

To create a wider ledge, build a frame parallel to the first

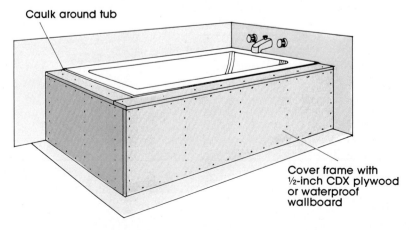

Caulk around tub

Cover frame with ½-inch CDX plywood or waterproof wallboard

INSTALLING
VANITY CABINETS

Vanity cabinets are generally open in back to accommodate plumbing. The installation of a vanity cabinet is a relatively simple job. Instructions for installing a counter top follow on page 78–79.

Tools: level; screwdriver; drill; C clamps if joining two or more cabinets.

Supplies: screws; toggle bolts; shims; sandpaper.

1. Be sure your floor is level. If it is not, add shims beneath the cabinet, wherever necessary, so that water does not pool at one end of your counter top or run off onto the floor. Use a level to check it. The walls behind and beside the cabinet ought to be smooth as well. Bulges will prevent the cabinet from setting flush. Most irregularities can simply be sanded down. If sanding will not suffice, you may need to add shims at the wall to make the cabinet level.

2. Vanity cabinets are made to a standard height of 30 inches. For most people this is a satisfactory height, but it can be surprisingly irritating for people who are much taller than average. You can raise the height of your vanity cabinet in one of four ways: (a) Use modular kitchen cabinets, which are 34½ inches high and 24 inches deep; (b) Build a plywood base for your cabinet with 2 by 4s; (c) Raise the

toe-kick; (d) Raise the counter top. To raise the toe-kick, place the cabinet upside down, and screw precisely measured strips of wood to the bottom of its base. To raise the counter top, install similar strips of wood to the top of the cabinet's base before you install the counter top. Finish the faces of the wood strips to match the rest of the cabinet, or add an extra-wide band of vinyl molding at the base.

Raising the Toe-Kick

Raising the Counter Top

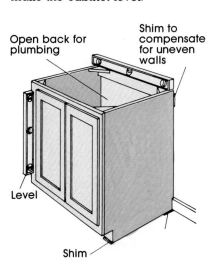

Open back for plumbing

Shim to compensate for uneven walls

Level

Shim

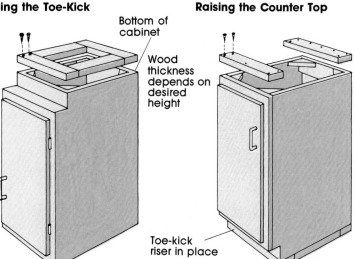

Bottom of cabinet

Wood thickness depends on desired height

Toe-kick riser in place

3. Attach your cabinet to the walls. Measure the height the cabinet should reach, and draw a line on the wall the length or depth of the cabinet to gauge your level and accuracy as you work. Screw through the cabinet's hanging strip into every stud, not simply into the wall's face; the weight of the cabinet should rest on the floor, not the screws.

4. If you are installing a series of adjacent units to make one long cabinet, clamp the units together with C clamps. Then drill pilot holes, and attach the units together with wood screws through adjoining stiles. Check the cabinet's

level periodically: Tightening screws will often pull a unit out of line. If this happens you may have to readjust, add, or subtract some shims.

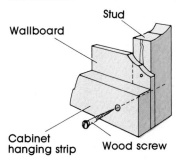

Stud

Wallboard

Cabinet hanging strip

Wood screw

Level

Pencil line

Shim

C clamp

Wall

Shim

WOOD COUNTER TOPS

A vanity may come with its own counter top, but you might choose to make your own. Because plastic laminate is more easily done by a professional, wood, ceramic tile, and cultured marble are the surfaces you are likely to do yourself. A tiled counter requires a ¾-inch plywood base, which is made the same way as a wood counter. Many brands of cultured marble cannot be worked with normal woodworking tools, but some, like Corian®, can. These are worked a little differently (see facing page). The first step in making your counter top is to measure carefully. The counter top should be 1 inch deeper than the cabinet to provide some front overhang. If the sides do not abut walls, plan a ½-inch overhang on each side. Before the completed counter top is installed, you will add a backsplash to prevent water from marring the walls and from seeping behind the cabinet. Your backsplash should be at least 4 inches high and as long as your counter top. If one side abuts a wall, plan a sidesplash as well. You can purchase wood in a large sheet and cut it at home, or prepare exact measurements and have it cut at the lumberyard.

Tools: circular saw; drill; saber saw.

Supplies: construction glue; 2d finishing nails; sandpaper; screws; silicone seal; Varathane (if wood surface); ¾-inch plywood to size.

1. Cut all materials to size, including the base, back-, and side-splashes. To double the thickness of the base for a substantial-looking wood counter or for face tiles, cut strips of wood, ¾ by 2 inches, and attach them all around the edges. Secure them with glue and 2d nails set about 2 inches apart. When the glue has dried, sand all the edges smooth. Then mark the position for the basin hole. Many manufacturers provide a template of the basin you buy, or you can use the basin itself. Turn it upside down in position, and trace the outline. Leave at least 2 inches of counter in front and behind the basin's rim.

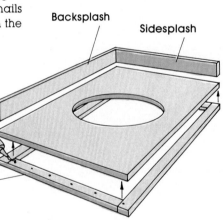

Backsplash

Sidesplash

Glue

Doubling strip, approximately ¾ by 2 inches

2. Cut the basin hole. Drill one starting hole immediately inside your outline if your basin is circular, or one hole inside each corner if it is square or rectangular. Use a saber saw to cut the basin hole, and stay inside the line or you may end up with a hole slightly larger than your basin. If you plan to cover the counter with tile, install the counter before laying the tiles.

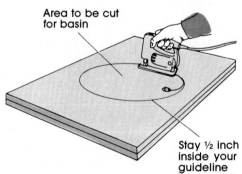

Area to be cut for basin

Stay ½ inch inside your guideline

3. Attach the backsplash to the back of the counter top, using a thick bead of silicone seal; then secure it from under the counter top with wood screws at 1- to 2-inch intervals. Drill pilot holes for the screws. Clean up excess sealant immediately.

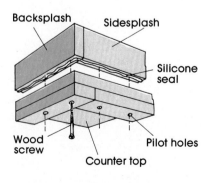

Backsplash

Sidesplash

Silicone seal

Wood screw

Pilot holes

Counter top

4. Attach the counter top to the vanity. It's easier to use glue than to insert wood screws, but the counter top will be easier to move in the future if you have to remove only the screws. If you are using hardwood for the counter surface itself, finish the wood with a liquid plastic such as Varathane.

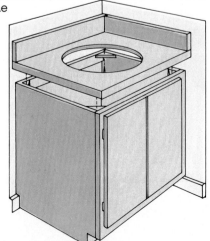

Set your counter top, and screw in place from beneath

INSTALLING
SYNTHETIC MARBLE COUNTERTOPS

As noted on page 39 most cultured marble cannot be worked with standard woodworking tools. Some brands, like Corian®, can be cut as long as your tools are equipped with carbide blades. The work may be harder than the simple instructions indicate, so don't undertake this yourself without a thorough understanding of the material and the process. The material is sold in ¼-inch-thick sheets, 30 inches wide by 57, 60, 72, 80, and 98 inches long; it is also sold in ½-inch-thick sheets 25 and 30 inches wide by 98 and 121 inches long. For the most part you install this counter top the same way you install a wood top, but it is very heavy; when working with it you should see that it is well supported at all times.

Tools: circular saw with carbide blade; router (optional); drill with carbide bit.

Supplies: goggles; dust mask; sandpaper; caulk; neoprene adhesive.

1. Measure and cut your counter top. Wear goggles and a dust mask, and use a carbide blade in a circular saw.

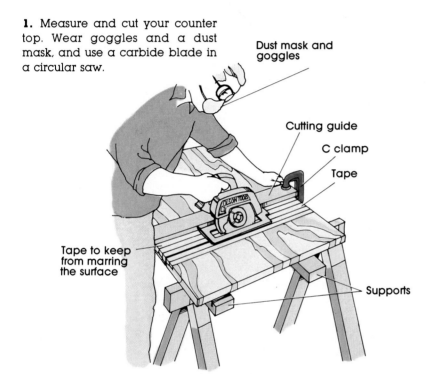

Dust mask and goggles

Cutting guide

C clamp

Tape

Tape to keep from marring the surface

Supports

2. Finish the edges by sanding them smooth or by carving decorative edges with a router.

Sample of edge styles available

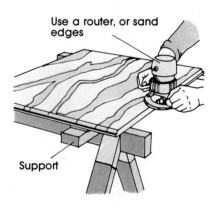

Use a router, or sand edges

Support

3. Mark and cut out your basin hole as with a standard counter-top core.

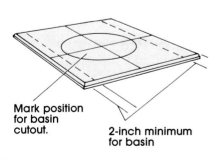

Mark position for basin cutout.

2-inch minimum for basin

4. Apply sealing caulk around the top edges of the vanity cabinet, set the counter top in place, and press it firmly into the caulk for about ten minutes.

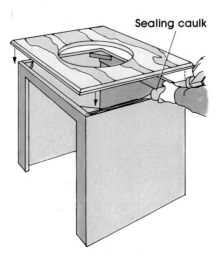

Sealing caulk

5. Attach the backsplash with a neoprene adhesive, caulk the juncture between the counter top and backsplash, and clean off any excess caulk.

Backsplash—attach with neoprene adhesive

Caulk here.

INSTALLING
TILE COUNTER TOPS

It's hard to beat the value of ceramic tiles. But because such a surface is liable to be as permanent as your bathroom, it demands a bit of extra planning. You'll need to make a plywood base as described on page 78. You may want to use cementboard instead of plywood.

Tools: notched trowel; tile saw; tile nippers; rubber trowel.

Supplies: mastic; grout; wet rag or sponge; buff cloth; grout sealer.

1. You do not need the thick tiles generally used for floors to cover your counter top, but shop around for high-quality tiles that are less likely to chip. Field tiles are used for everything but the edges and are sold by the square foot. Bullnose tiles, which have one rounded edge, are used at the front and side edges of your counter top and are sold by the linear foot. There are other special tiles—quarter-round and cove tiles, for example—and you should be aware of which ones are available in your chosen style. Measure the width and depth of your plywood base, including back- and sidesplashes, and then measure the tiles you want to buy. Calculate the number of tiles you will need. Buy a few extra tiles of each type so you can replace any that become damaged.

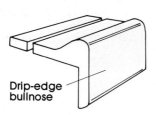

Drip-edge bullnose

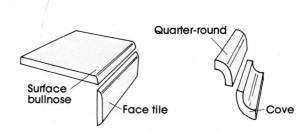

Surface bullnose · Face tile · Quarter-round · Cove

2. Lay out your pattern. Start with an outside edge and position all your bullnose tiles for the front and side edges. Make adjustments to limit the cuts and to place the cuts where you want them.

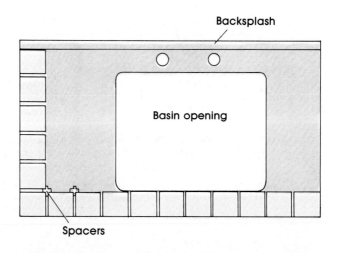

Backsplash

Basin opening

Spacers

3. When you're satisfied with the cuts along the back- and side-splashes, lay out the tiles around the basin. If you have a self-rimming or flush-mounted basin with a metal rim, you can lay each tile over the edge of the basin cutout, mark each one for its cut, and use a tile cutter or nippers to cut them all back. The basin will cover the raw edges. If you have a recessed basin, you'll need to be more precise, planning cove tiles and an even grout line around the rim.

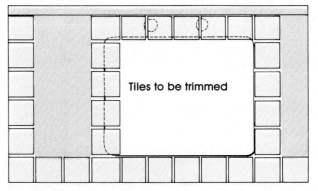

Tiles to be trimmed

4. When you know where all your tiles will go, mark tiles, counter, or both, to guide you in tricky areas; make your tile cuts, and prepare to set your tiles. Use a notched trowel to spread a thin layer of mastic or epoxy over a small portion of your counter top. Hold the trowel at about a 45° angle to achieve maximum coverage. Different adhesives take different amounts of time to dry, so follow the manufacturer's advice carefully. Do not cover a larger area than you can tile easily before the glue is too dry to hold the tiles.

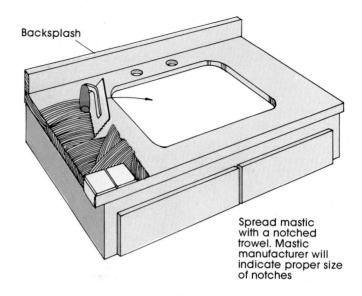

Backsplash

Spread mastic with a notched trowel. Mastic manufacturer will indicate proper size of notches

5. Starting with the face tiles on the edge and bullnose tiles at the front of your counter top, lay the tiles on, one small area at a time. Place each tile carefully, and press it down, twisting slightly as you set it into place. Using the edges of the counter for guidance, make sure your lines stay straight. When necessary, use tile nippers to cut tiles to fit. Work your way up the backsplash, ending with a row of bullnose tiles for the backsplash's top edge. Remove excess mastic from the tiles, and let the whole project set overnight, or as long as the manufacturer recommends.

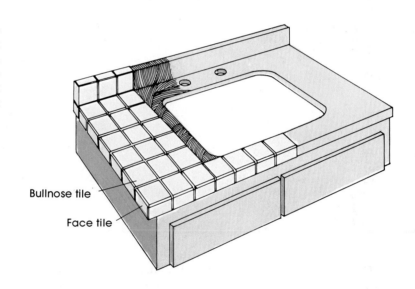

Bullnose tile

Face tile

6. Use a rubber trowel to spread grout over the tile according to the grout manufacturer's instructions. Be sure to press the grout into the crevices between tiles. There are tools for this, but many people just use the end of a toothbrush to get a smooth finish. Clean off excess grout with a wet rag or sponge. When the surface grout has dried, buff the tile with a dry cloth. In two to three weeks, when the grout has cured completely, apply a tile grout sealer to keep it clean and mildew-free.

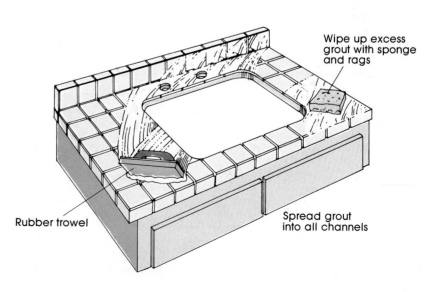

Wipe up excess grout with sponge and rags

Rubber trowel

Spread grout into all channels

INSTALLING
WASHBASINS

Ordinarily, you will purchase fittings separately from the basin itself, and the manufacturer will provide instructions for assembly. You may find that your new basin does not align exactly with the old supply and drain lines. Many hardware stores, plumbing supply outlets, and home improvement centers carry the flexible copper and plastic pipes that allow you to accommodate a fixture that is a little out of synch with your old plumbing. You can also attach shutoff valves to these lines if your plumbing lines do not already have them. Usually, you will install your vanity cabinet before hanging or setting the fixture itself (see page 77). Because part of the basin

installation then occurs in cramped under-the-counter conditions, you can make your task easier by attaching as many of the fittings as possible before installing the basin. If you're going to install shutoff valves, do this before installing the basin as well.

Tools: screwdriver; wrench; plumber's (basin) wrench; level.

Supplies: plumber's putty; mounting clips for inset basin; brackets for wall-mounted basin; flexible supply line connectors and shutoff valves if necessary; hardware and fittings; joint tape or compound; caulk.

1. Attach the fittings. Set your basin on its side so you can reach the top and bottom at once. Run a string of plumber's putty ⅛ to ¼ inch wide on the bottom of the faucet/spout fitting, and push the mechanism firmly into place. From under the basin, attach the washers and retaining nuts to the fitting's stems, and tighten them, being careful not to crack or chip the basin.

2. Connect the water supply lines to the faucets, but not to the stubouts. Run a string of plumber's putty

around the drain post, and push that post firmly into the drain hole, securing it with washers and nuts.

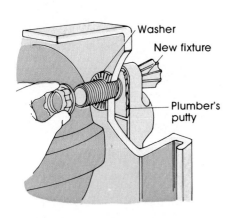

- Washer
- New fixture
- Plumber's putty

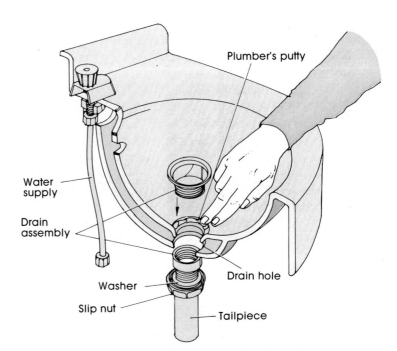

- Plumber's putty
- Water supply
- Drain assembly
- Drain hole
- Washer
- Slip nut
- Tailpiece

3. If you are installing a counter-top basin, run another string of plumber's putty around the rim of the counter-top hole, and set the basin in place, supporting it from underneath. Straighten it, using a level. Then, from under the basin, slide six to twelve evenly spaced mounting clips into place on the basin's rim so that they grip the bottom of the counter top, and tighten.

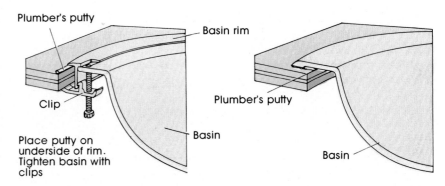

- Plumber's putty
- Basin rim
- Clip
- Basin
- Plumber's putty
- Basin

Place putty on underside of rim. Tighten basin with clips

4. If you are installing a wall-mounted basin, install the hanger brackets on the wall according to the manufacturer's instructions; then lower the basin over the hanger brackets, and straighten it with a level.

Three Common Types of Wall Hangers

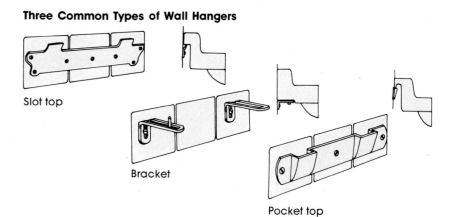

Slot top

Bracket

Pocket top

5. Connect the water supply lines to the stub-outs. Then connect the drain assembly. If your faucet has a pop-up drain assembly, it is contained in a T-drain. Install the stopper control above the drain tail pipe with the pivot rod pointing to the rear wall. Attach the pivot rod through the clevis with a spring clip. The clevis is attached to the lift-up control; the pop-up drain plug is secured to the pivot rod inside the drain. Work the plunger several times to make sure it opens and closes adequately.

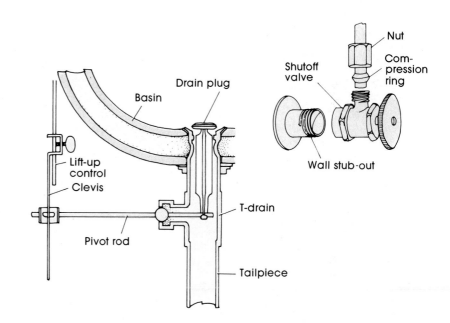

Drain plug

Basin

Nut

Shutoff valve

Compression ring

Lift-up control

Clevis

Wall stub-out

T-drain

Pivot rod

Tailpiece

6. Attach the p-trap to the drainpipe with a slip nut and washer, and secure it tightly. Then attach the p-trap to the drain tail pipe with a slip nut and washer, and attach that tightly. Open both the hot and cold shutoff valves, and open the faucets. Make sure everything is working properly. If you see any leaks, tighten the appropriate nut until the leaking stops.

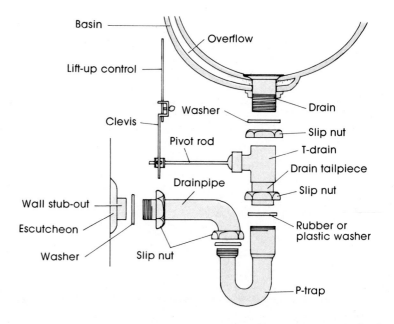

Basin

Overflow

Lift-up control

Washer

Drain

Clevis

Slip nut

Pivot rod

T-drain

Drainpipe

Drain tailpiece

Wall stub-out

Slip nut

Escutcheon

Rubber or plastic washer

Washer

Slip nut

P-trap

INSTALLING
TILE WALLS

Basically, a wall of tiles consists of an area of full-size field tiles and a border of the same or different tiles. Because it is rare for tiles to fit a space exactly, you need to figure out how many full tiles will fit and what you're going to do with the odd spaces that are left. To make these decisions you need to plot your pattern on the wall. Start by measuring the height and width of each wall you plan to cover, and the size of the tiles you're going to use. Using these measurements, determine the approximate number of tiles you'll need. Measure trim pieces separately. To plot a tile pattern, professional tile setters often use a pair of compass dividers and a pair of layout rods. These rods are strips of 1 by 1, one cut to the length of your wall and the other to its height. The steps that follow use this method.

Tools: plumb line; straightedge; compass dividers; two layout rods; tile cutter; tile nippers; level; notched trowel; rubber trowel.

Supplies: field and border tiles; mastic; grout; wet rag or sponge; buff cloth; grout sealer.

1. Measure the width of your wall. At the center, drop a plumb line from the ceiling to the floor, and use it to draw a straight vertical line. Drop two more plumb lines close to the edges of the wall. Measure the height of your wall, and draw an exact horizontal line across the wall at the center. Check the angles it makes with your vertical lines. They should be exactly 90°. Draw two more horizontal lines as close to the floor and ceiling as possible. Check their angles. If the outside lines show that your floor, ceiling, or walls are uneven, plan to fill in these wedgelike spaces.

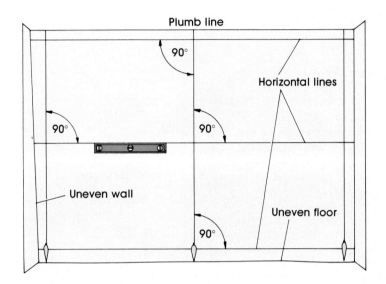

2. Next, set the points of your compass divider at the width of your tile. If the tile has a small protruding lip on the bottom, it has been preformed to include a grout space. If it has no such lip, add no less than 1/16 inch and no more than 3/16 inch to your measurement to accommodate grout. Then walk your compass along the height layout rod, marking as you go. Chances are, the last space on the rod will not be the exact width of a full tile. You can leave that space and put a cut tile at the top or bottom of your wall, or you can adjust all your tiles so you'll have cut tiles of equal size at both top and bottom (see Step 3).

3. If you want equal-size cut tiles at top and bottom, measure the last space, add the width of a full tile, and divide that measurement in half. Turn your layout rod over and mark that distance on each end. Then reset your compass dividers to the full width of tile and grout lines, and walk them along the rod again. The measurements should fit exactly between the ends. Hold the rod beside two of your plumb lines, and transfer your markings to the wall.

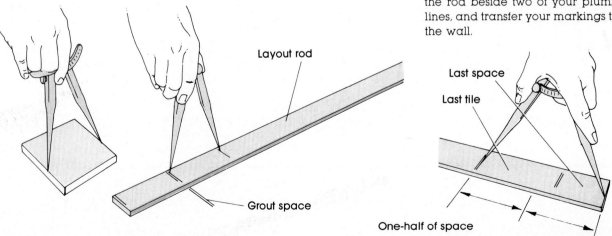

Layout rod

Grout space

Last space

Last tile

One-half of space

Plumb line

90°

Horizontal lines

90°

90°

Uneven wall

90°

Uneven floor

4. If you're using special border tiles or trim pieces, start by measuring their width (including space for grout) on one or both ends of your layout rod, according to your design. Then measure off the full tiles between your border markings. If they don't come out even, which they probably won't, decide how you want to adjust the tiles. You can widen the border and add a cut border tile; you can cut one or two of your field tiles; or you can make your grout lines a little wider or narrower. Whatever you decide, mark the measurements on your layout rod and transfer them to two of your vertical lines on the wall. Follow Steps 2–4 for your horizontal layout rod. Transfer the marks to two of the horizontal lines on the wall. If you want, draw a complete grid on the wall, following the hatchmarks you've made.

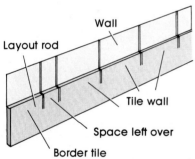

6. To work around any irregularity such as a faucet, cut a tile into two pieces. Use a glass cutter to score the glazed side of the tile. Lay the unglazed side on a nail placed directly under the score, press firmly on the edges of the tile, and break it. Mark both parts of your cutout with a grease pencil, trim with tile nippers, and set the pieces in place.

5. When your measurements are complete, begin to set your tiles. Start with the first horizontal row of full tiles, leaving the borders, trim pieces, or cut tiles for the end. Use a notched trowel and whatever mastic the tile manufacturer recommends. Mastic sets quickly and will not accept tiles once it begins to harden, so cover only small areas

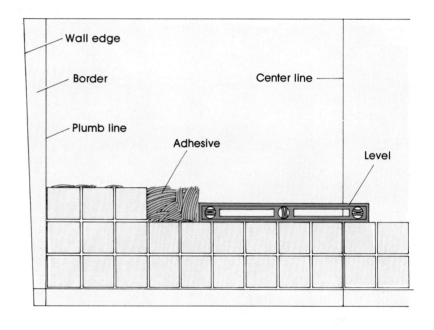

7. When your field tiles are in place, set your border, trim, and cut tiles. For any cut tiles, place a full tile upside down over the gap to be filled. Leaving space for grout lines on both sides, mark the edge to be cut, and cut as described in Step 6. Spread the cut tile with adhesive, and set it in place, cut side out.

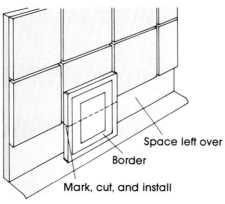

at a time. Do not apply any mastic over your first plumb or horizontal lines—you can use these as guides. Lay the tiles down one at a time, twisting each one slightly to embed it in the mastic, and remove excess mastic from the face of the tiles. Check each row with a level, and proceed up the wall one row at a time until the wall is tiled.

8. Allow the mastic to dry as long as the manufacturer recommends. Then spread grout over the wall with a rubber trowel. Press the grout into the crevices with the rounded end of a stick or toothbrush. Clean off the excess grout with a wet rag or sponge. When the grout is dry, buff the tile with a dry cloth. When the grout has cured completely, apply a grout sealer to keep it clean and mildew-free.

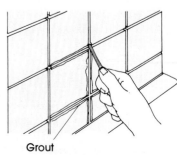

TILE FLOORS

Floor tiles are generally thicker than counter-top tiles; therefore, if you have many large or straight cuts to make, you may want to rent a commercial tile cutter. Tile nippers will suffice for small trim jobs, but not for the big ones. Always wear goggles to protect your eyes when cutting tiles since the chips do fly. Most floor tiles do not come with special trim pieces, which you may not need anyway. If you want baseboards or molding, you can choose any that seem to fit your design.

When you've selected and purchased your tiles, plan your pattern. You can establish your pattern by following Steps 1 through 3 for Vinyl Floor Tiles on page 90 or by following the steps outlined here. When you plan your pattern, you are deciding where you want to place the cut pieces around the edges of the room and how equal you want them to be. The steps on page 90 sug-

gest centering tiles in the middle of the room and shifting the rows so that a cut tile on one end is balanced by a cut tile of equal size on the other. The method outlined here suggests establishing a row centered in the doorway. With this method you always start with full tiles at the doorway and may have cut tiles at the other end. You can try either or both ways and decide which looks better. Make sure your floor surface is clean, dry, and flat. Sand rough surfaces, and, if necessary, install new underlayment.

Tools: tile cutter; tile nippers; chalk line; two wood strips; hammer; unnotched trowel; notched trowel; rubber trowel; roller; carpet-wrapped length of 2 by 4; mallet.

Supplies: goggles; sandpaper; mastic; nails; grout; damp cloth or sponge; buff cloth; tile sealer.

1. Measure the width of your bathroom doorway, and mark its center. Snap a chalk line from this point to the back of the room, making sure that it is exactly perpendicular to the threshold. Following the line, lay out full tiles from the doorway to the other end, leaving 1/16 inch between them—use

spacers. When you've laid as many full tiles as you can, draw a line on the floor to mark the back edge of the last tile. Nail a wood strip across the end of the room so that its inside edge meets your mark, is exactly perpendicular to your chalk line, and runs the full width of the bathroom. This strip must be straight

even if the back wall is not. Then lay out a horizontal row of tiles. Wherever the last full tile ends, nail down another wood strip perpendicular to the first. The two wood strips must form a perfect 90° angle, because you will begin setting tiles in this corner and your rows must be perfectly straight.

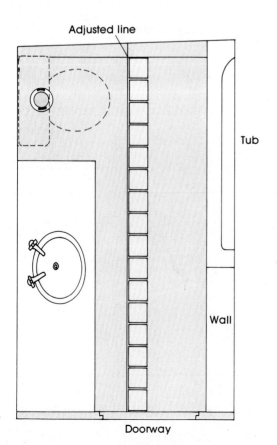

Adjusted line

Tub

Wall

Doorway

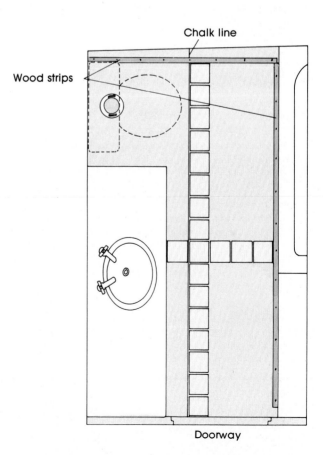

Chalk line

Wood strips

Doorway

2. Beginning at your square corner, apply the adhesive recommended by the tile manufacturer or your dealer. Plan to apply two coats of adhesive. Spread the first coat with an unnotched trowel, covering the floor completely. This coat ensures a good bond and helps waterproof the underlayment. With a notched trowel held at a 45° angle, apply the second coat, covering one 3-foot-square section at a time.

3. Starting in the corner press each tile into place. Twist it a little to help it adhere, but don't slide it around in the glue too much. Insert 1/16-inch spacers between the tiles. Keep excess adhesive cleaned out of the grout channels and off the face of the tiles. When you finish tiling the first section, continue with an adjacent section until the floor is covered with all the full tiles.

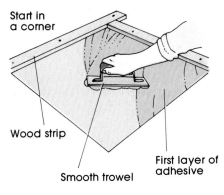

Start in a corner

Wood strip

Smooth trowel

First layer of adhesive

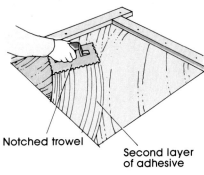

Notched trowel

Second layer of adhesive

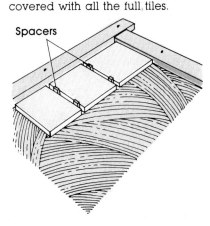

Spacers

4. When the full tiles are all in place, remove the two wood strips. Cut tiles to fit around fixtures and the edge of the floor. To cut a tile, turn a full tile upside down and slide it over the space to be filled. (You turn it upside down because you want the cut edge to face the wall. When you flip the cut tile over, it should fit perfectly, accommodating any odd shapes due to irregularities in the wall.) Mark it on both edges, allowing 1/16 inch for the grout line. Turn it over, run the mark across the face of the tile, and cut it with your tile cutter. Cut all your odd-shaped tiles in this way, keeping track of which tiles go where, and then set them with adhesive. Apply adhesive to the floor with a smooth trowel and to the back of the tile with a notched trowel. Press the tiles into place.

5. Your tiles will set more successfully and evenly if you press the entire surface down with a roller within a couple of hours after the installation is complete. For hard-to-reach places use a length of 2 by 4 covered with scrap carpet or rags, and tap it gently with a mallet.

6. After the adhesive has set for 24 hours, apply grout with a rubber trowel. Clean out excess grout at the corners with a rounded stick or the end of a toothbrush. Remove excess grout from the face of the tile with a damp cloth or sponge, and then buff the tiles with a dry cloth. One to two weeks after the grout has cured, apply a tile sealer over all the grouted joints to keep them clean and to prevent mildew.

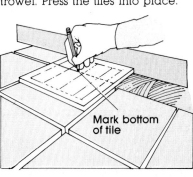

Mark bottom of tile

2 by 4 wrapped in scrap carpeting

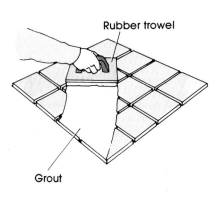

Rubber trowel

Grout

INSTALLING
MOSAIC TILES

In addition to individual tiles, ceramic tile is also available in sheets made up of smaller, "mosaic" tiles. Some sheets are pregrouted; others are held together with paper on the face of the tiles or mesh on the back. In either case prepare your floor surface as outlined in Steps 1 through 3 for installing Ceramic Floor Tiles.

Tools: utility knife or razor blade; tile nippers; rubber trowel.

Supplies: mastic; grout; damp cloth or sponge; buff cloth.

1. When laying a sheet of ceramic tiles, fold, bend, or roll the sheet inward so that the tile face is hidden. Set the open end of the sheet in place on the adhesive, and slowly unfold the sheet, pressing the tiles into the glue as you work. The space between sheets should equal the space between the tiles.

2. When you work around an obstruction of some sort, use a utility knife or razor blade to cut along the seams in the sheet, removing all the tiles affected by the obstacle. Use tile nippers to cut individual tiles to fit around the obstruction.

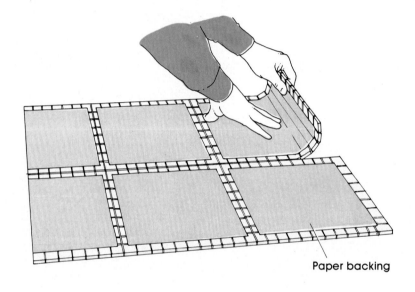

Paper backing

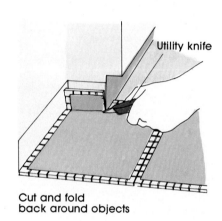

Utility knife

Cut and fold
back around objects

3. To fill border spaces turn the sheet over, slide it over the space, and mark it. Cut along the line.

4. Apply adhesive to the floor and the back of the sheet, and press the trimmed sheet into place. If the face of your tiles is covered with protective paper, soak the paper with warm water, and peel it off.

5. Use a rubber trowel to spread grout into all the junctures. Wipe off the excess grout with a damp cloth or sponge, and buff the tiles with a dry cloth.

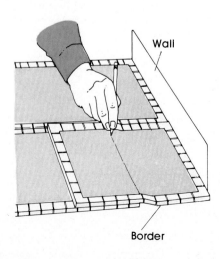

Wall

Border

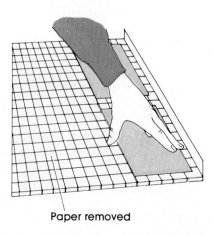

Paper removed

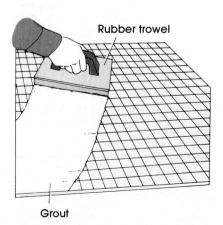

Rubber trowel

Grout

INSTALLING
SHEET VINYL & CARPET

You must have a smooth subfloor before installing sheet vinyl, because the material conforms to the floor beneath it. Bumps and bulges will show and may eventually damage the vinyl. Installing sheet vinyl is a bit trickier than vinyl tiles (see pages 90–91) because of the painstaking care required to ensure accurate cutouts around fixtures and corners, and because a full roll of the material is heavy and unwieldy. Nonetheless, loosely laid (no adhesive) sheet vinyl offers so wide a variety of flooring possibilities at a moderate price that it is very popular in bathrooms. Try to select a roll width that will not require butting two sheets together. A bathroom is rarely so long or wide that it cannot be covered by a single width. The easiest way to cut your sheet to size is to unroll it in another room, and draw your bathroom layout directly on the vinyl. Laying carpet is much the same as laying vinyl, but it's easier. Because carpet is flexible, you can make your cuts more easily. Follow the steps below.

Tools: utility knife; trowel; straightedge.

Supplies: mastic.

1. Carefully measure your bathroom floor. Measurements around fixtures, curves, and corners should be very precise. If you're worried about accuracy, lay out a paper pattern: Cut and tape pieces of paper together until they entirely cover the floor.

2. Transfer your measured outline or paper pattern to the unrolled vinyl. When you've drawn your outline, place a thick piece of cardboard under the area you want to cut, to protect your floor and knife blade. Using a utility knife, cut around the outline, leaving 3 to 6 inches of extra vinyl on all sides. This allows for errors and stretching, and you can trim away the extra when you have laid the flooring.

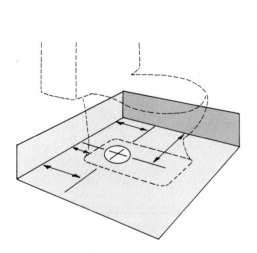

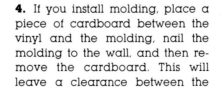
Paper pattern

Leave approximately
3 inches for errors
and stretching

3. Move the sheet to your bathroom, and lay it out. Trim large overlaps immediately with your utility knife. Then trim precisely, leaving a minimum gap of ⅛ inch between the vinyl and the wall. This allows for expansion and contraction of the underlayment. Molding will cover the gap.

4. If you install molding, place a piece of cardboard between the vinyl and the molding, nail the molding to the wall, and then remove the cardboard. This will leave a clearance between the molding and the floor, which allows the walls and floor to shift without affecting the vinyl. Install a threshold at the doorway to protect that edge.

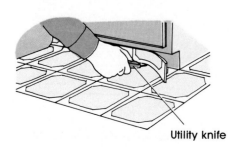
Utility knife

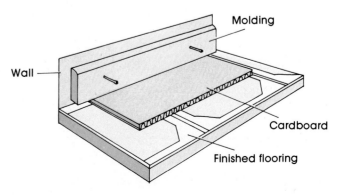
Molding

Wall

Cardboard

Finished flooring

INSTALLING
VINYL FLOOR TILES

Vinyl tiles conform to the surface they overlay: Bumps, bulges, or other irregularities in the underlayment will show through and interfere with adhesion, preventing tiles from lying flat and causing them to come unglued in the future. Therefore, you must smooth the existing underlayment or replace it.

Vinyl tiles are generally much easier to lay than sheet vinyl, because you don't have to handle a large roll of material, and you can make cutouts on the spot using a utility knife or even a pair of heavy-duty shears. The disadvantage of vinyl tiles, apart from their being somewhat more expensive than sheet vinyl, is that if the tiles become loose water can seep between them and

rot the underlayment. But carefully installed vinyl tiles should serve you well. The method shown here for laying out your tiles is not the only one. See also pages 86–87 on ceramic floor tiles. Basically you're trying to determine where you'll place cut tiles. You may want a full tile near the door or along the tub, for instance. By laying out the tiles you can decide what you like and then determine which method will ensure straight, even rows when you set them.

Tools: chalk line or straightedge and chalk; utility knife.

Supplies: mastic; silicone seal.

1. Determine the center of all four bathroom walls, and draw lines on the floor connecting the center points. Snap a chalk line or use a straightedge and a piece of loose chalk. The point at which the two lines intersect, forming four 90° angles, is the center of your bathroom.

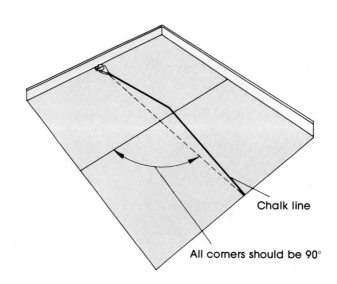

Chalk line

All corners should be 90°

2. To achieve even rows of tile with identical borders, lay one full row of tiles along either line, from wall to wall, without applying any adhesive. If, when you reach the end of your trial row, a space remains that is smaller than half the width of a single tile, remove the last tile. Measure the new space and divide the measurement by 2. Return to the beginning of your row and move the first tile up as many inches as your answer; you will now have equal spaces at each end of the row, and each will be smaller than one full tile. (Example: You are using 12-inch tiles; the space remaining at the end of the row is 1 inch. When you remove a tile you have a total of 13 inches of space. Divide by 2, which equals 6½ inches. By restarting your row 6½ inches from the wall, you will also have 6½ inches at the other end of

the row.) If, when you reach the end of your trial row, a space remains that is larger than half the width of a single tile, leave it. A single end row more than half the width of a tile will not stand out or look bad.

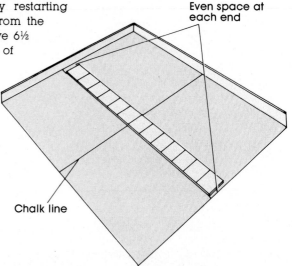

Even space at each end

Chalk line

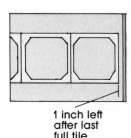

1 inch left after last full tile

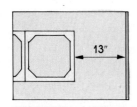

13″

Remove last tile, divide the new space by two, and adjust entire row to leave 6½ inches at either end.

3. With the first row in place, set out a trial row of tiles perpendicular to it, as close to your second chalked line as possible, but fit so the sides of the center tiles meet exactly. If you have to move this second row to create even end tiles, do so. Then slide the entire first row to the left or right until the rows are completely aligned.

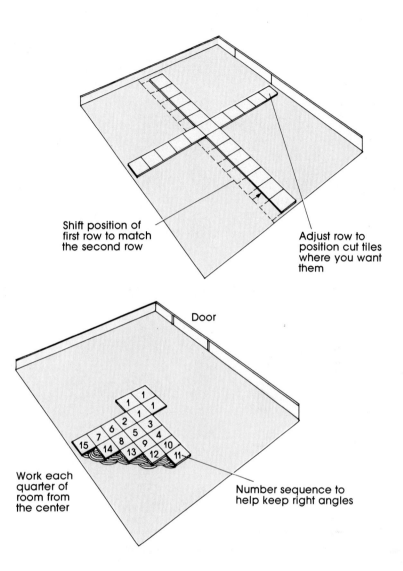

Shift position of first row to match the second row

Adjust row to position cut tiles where you want them

4. Using the adhesive recommended by the tile manufacturer, set your four center tiles in place. Remember that mastics used on floors harden quickly, so cover only a small portion of your floor at a time. Then start with the quarter of the room farthest from the door, and fill in that section of the floor first. Use only full tiles, and work toward the walls in sequence as shown. Cut tiles to fit around obstacles such as pipes or fixtures that are already in place.

Door

Work each quarter of room from the center

Number sequence to help keep right angles

5. Do all the border tiles last. Turn one full tile upside down, lay it over the gap between the wall and your covered floor, and cut it where it overlaps the tile you've laid. This will give your border tiles an exact fit with the wall. Measure and cut each border tile separately in case your wall is not straight. Complete each quarter of the floor in the same way as the first. Apply silicone seal around the bases of all fixtures. You should be able to walk on your floor within 24 hours.

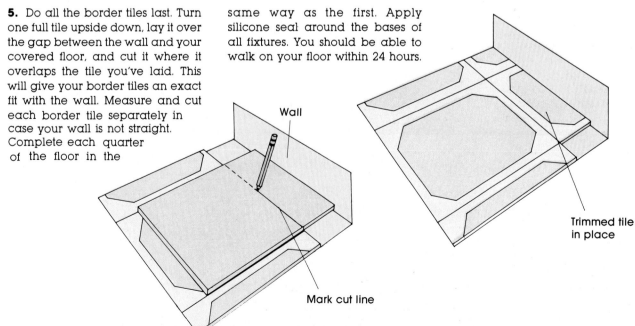

Wall

Mark cut line

Trimmed tile in place

INSTALLING
TOILETS

Installing a toilet is usually the last major job in remodeling a bathroom. It is as simple as removing a toilet. Depending on the style you buy, there will be variations in the particulars of installation. Follow the manufacturer's instructions.

Tools: level; wrench.

Supplies: old towels; wax gasket; plastic gasket sleeve (if necessary); plumber's putty; joint compound or joint tape.

1. Resting it on some old towels or bath mats to protect its surface, turn your new toilet upside down and place a round wax gasket around the drain hole, pushing it down firmly all around. No gasket comes with your toilet; you'll have to buy one at the hardware store, but it will cost only a few dollars. If you have installed a new subfloor, it may be higher than your existing flange. If so, you can buy a wax gasket with a plastic sleeve that will make up the distance.

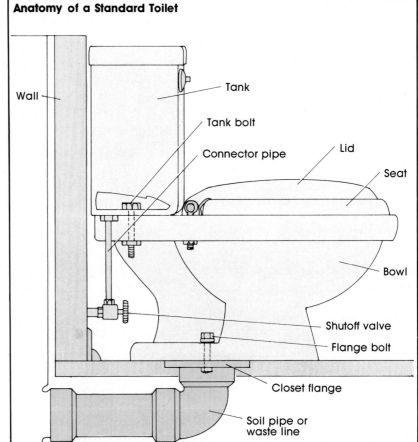

Anatomy of a Standard Toilet

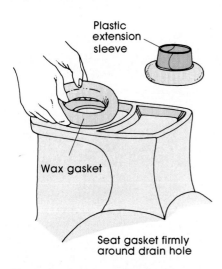

Seat gasket firmly around drain hole

2. If you have relocated your toilet, you will have to install the closet flange on the new waste pipe. Following the manufacturer's instructions, install the flange so that it is flush with the underlayment.

3. Remove the rags from your drainpipe. Turn the toilet right side up, and set it down over the drain hole with the flange bolts protruding up through the flanges on both sides. Grasping the bowl rim on either side, press the bowl to the floor. Twist and rock it gently back and forth as you go, to assure a complete seal with the wax gasket. Do not lift the bowl or you will break the seal.

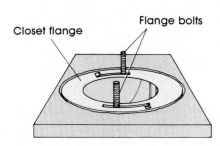

4. Use a level to make sure the bowl is correctly aligned in both directions. Then put washers on the flange bolts, and tighten the nuts until the bowl does not rock. Cover the bolts with plastic or ceramic caps. The caps are usually purchased separately for most standard-design toilets. If you have purchased a special color or a nonstandard design, the caps are usually part of the package.

5. Install the tank according to the manufacturer's directions. Make sure it is aligned with the bowl's rim so that the tank bolts can connect the two parts of the unit. The bolts should be in place, and the nuts aligned, before the flushing assembly is connected.

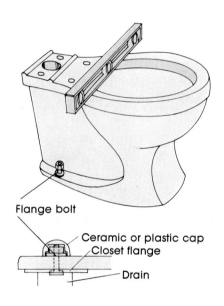

Flange bolt

Ceramic or plastic cap
Closet flange
Drain

Tank

Bolts

Rubber washer

Cone-shape gasket

Rubber cushion

Washer and nut

6. Attach the flexible water supply line to the flush valve stem by tightening the coupling nuts. Turn on the water supply, and watch for leaks while the tank fills. When the tank is full, flush the toilet several times, examining the base of the bowl to be certain the gasket is not leaking. If water appears, tighten the flange bolts, mop up the water, and try again. If more water appears, your seal is

broken or defective. You will have to drain the toilet and tank, turn off the water supply, remove the toilet, and reset it with a new gasket.

7. If there is no leak, as will probably be the case, install the toilet seat by fitting the seat bolts into the holes at the back of the bowl's rim, and secure the bolts with washers and nuts.

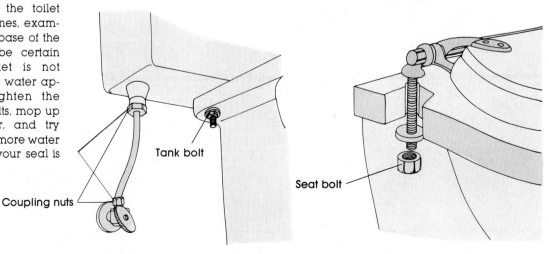

Coupling nuts

Tank bolt

Seat bolt

FINISHING TOUCHES

Your finished bathroom is ultimately the result of your decisions about both design and style. While the basic design determines the layout and establishes the lines and scale of the room, your choices of materials, accessories, finishes, and personal belongings set the tone.

In this rectangular bathroom, one major design decision—to install the large window at the end of the room—totally alters the look of the bathroom. Opening up the rear wall and ceiling, the window floods the room with natural light and lends a dramatic touch to its plain contours. Pale blue walls set the color scheme, which is carried out with deep blue tiles and bright blue towels.

Then style steps in. The old-fashioned shower fitting immediately establishes that this bathroom combines both the old and the new. This theme is carried out by the unusual wall piece over the vanity. Constructed of molding, panels, and turned-wood trimmings, the structure has a turn-of-the-century air appropriate to the shower fitting. The curved basin fittings echo the line of the shower as well. These elaborate shapes, along with the intricately patterned Oriental rug, soften the severity of the rectilinear room.

Finally, the room is personalized by the belongings of the person who uses it: flowers and plants, which contribute a bit of color, a collection of seashells, and straw hats, which add a touch of whimsy. Some bathrooms are so sleek in their structural design that finishing touches may consist primarily of close attention to the details of essential accessories and hardware. Others, like the one pictured on these two pages, might look barren without the addition of personal belongings. The important point is that your bathroom remodeling is actually complete only when you've focused your attention on these last details—details that can finish (or undo) all the work that has preceded them. When your new bathroom finally reflects your personal touch, in whatever form that might take, your design actually comes to life.

Acknowledgments

Front Cover Photograph

Fred Lyon
Sausalito, CA

Photographic Locations

Diane Saeks
San Francisco, CA

Bathroom Design and Construction

Pages 1 and 24

Lambert Woods Architects
San Francisco, CA

Pages 4, 20, 54, 94, and 95

Sandra York
Interior Design
San Francisco, CA

Page 4

Oronato Associates, Inc.
Architect
Mountain View, CA

Pages 7 and 21

Suzanne Brangham Interiors
San Francisco, CA

Pages 14, 15, and 68

Emminger Woodworking and Construction
Lafayette, CA

Page 16

Jois
Interior Design
San Francisco, CA

Page 17, upper

Gutkin/Doubleday
Design
San Francisco, CA

Page 17, lower

Alan Lucas
Interior Design/Space Planning
Los Altos, CA

Page 18

Olivieri-Quinn Associates
Interior Design
San Francisco, CA

Page 19 and Back Cover

Diane Snow Crocker
Architectural and Interior Design
Lafayette, CA

Pages 22 and 23

William Duval Associates
Architects
San Francisco, CA

Anibal Davila
Contractor
San Francisco, CA

Towels

Lenore Linens
San Francisco, CA

Special Thanks to:

Jois Belfield
Suzanne Brangham
Ken Burke
Vicki Doubleday and Peter Gutkin
Hermitage House
Mrs. Richard Hoag
Sima Krames
Jose Lambert
Alan Lucas
Marion Makowsky
Betsy and David Morganthaler
Elizabeth Nelson
Maria Olivieri Quinn
Dr. Ralph Singer
Jodie Smith
Penny Westphal
Sandra York

Contractors and Technical Consultants

Pat Brook
Pleasant Hill, CA

Russell Coons
San Francisco, CA

Steve Crocker
Lafayette, CA

John Palmer
San Francisco, CA

Rick Sambol
Novato, CA

Interior Design Consultants

Diane Snow Crocker
Lafayette, CA

Diane Weinstein
Lafayette, CA

Editorial Research and Assistance

Karin Shakery
Darcie Furlan
Ami Zwicker

Copyediting

Editcetera
Berkeley, CA

Proofreading

Evelyn Spire
San Francisco, CA

Graphic Design Assistants

Cheryl Crockett
Ann Shumway
Polly Christiansen

Illustration Assistants

Marilyn Hill
Carla Simmons

Typesetting

Lehmann Graphics
Burlingame, CA

Color Separation

Color Tech
Redwood City, CA